"Imagine, mother, that you are to stay at home
and I am to travel into strange lands.
Imagine that my boat is ready
at the landing fully laden.
Now, think well, mother, before you say
what I shall bring for you
when I come back."

- Rabindranath Tagore, <u>The Crescent Moon</u>

Collections of Poetry in English

Blunderbuss(1971)

Apu's Initiation(1974)

Tomcat(1980)

The Hiroshima Clock(1990)

Coda(2022)

Canary Hill(2025)

CANARY HILL

Selected poetry 1971-2024
a sixth volume of verse

by

RUPENDRA GUHA MAJUMDAR

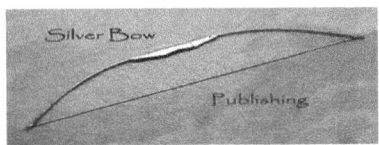

SILVER BOW PUBLISHING
720 SIXTH STREET, UNIT #5
NEW WESTMINSTER, BC
CANADA V3L 3C5

Title: CANARY HILL
Author: Rupendra Guha Majumdar
Cover art/sculpture: Rupendra Guha Majumdar
Cover composition: Mrittunjoy Guha Majumdar
All interior Illustrations: Rupendra Guha Majumdar
Layout and Design: Candice James
Editor: Candice James

All rights reserved including the right to reproduce or translate this book or any portions thereof, in any form without the permission of the publisher. Except for the use of short passages for review purposes, no part of this book may be reproduced, in part or in whole, or transmitted in any form or by any means, electronically or mechanically, including photocopying, recording, or any information or storage retrieval system without prior permission in writing from the publisher or a licence from the Canadian Copyright Collective Agency (Access Copyright).

© Silver Bow Publishing 2024
ISBN: 9781774033395 print book
ISBN: 9781774033401 e book

Library and Archives Canada Cataloguing in Publication

Title: Canary Hill : selected poetry 1971-2024, a sixth volume of verse / by Rupendra Guha Majumdar.
Other titles: Canary Hill (Compilation)
Names: Guha Majumdar, Rupendra, author. | Container of (work): Guha Majumdar, Rupendra. Bangladesh
   war and the cynic's epilogue.
Identifiers: Canadiana (print) 20240537742 | Canadiana (ebook) 20240537785 | ISBN 9781774033395
   (softcover) | ISBN 9781774033401 (Kindle)
Subjects: LCGFT: Poetry.
Classification: LCC PR9499.3.G69 C36 2024 | DDC 821/.914—dc23

To
revered guru
Sree Ma Anandamayee Ma
(1896-1982)
Of Kheora and Kankhal

"la fleur la plus parfaite que le sol

l'Inde ait produite"

votary of the music of the spirit
of the eternal rhythm
of
being and becoming

A REVIEW OF
'Searching For an E-book in the Spring'

The poem, 'Searching For an E-book in the Spring' in the volume, starts off lightly, facetiously, wittily, but then develops a remarkable depth. The poet's knowledge of Greek mythology is solid and that section is well handled. At first one was not sure what Guha-Majumdar was aiming at in his discussion of Darwin and 'ebok': what was likely to go extinct? Google? Ebooks? (The pun ebook-ebok suggested as much; the other pun, Gutenberg-Guten the Borg is lovely!). The new technology? All of the above? Obviously not Greek myths, since they are living, certainly for the poet and the reader too. But then one realizes that the poet has cast intimations of this extinction quite early. To begin with, the software program is confused and then, it just lapses into silence: it cannot cope. So it turns out to be like the ebok which, even at the point of extinction, calls "ebok, ebok!" but the point is that its cries are mute. I think the use and placement of that word is remarkably sophisticated and astute. A fine poem.

~ **Brij Raj Singh, Former Professor of English, Delhi University; Professor (Emeritus), Hostos Community College; the City University of New York, USA.**

FOREWORD

Rupendra Guha Majumdar has been writing poetry for the more than fifty years during which he has published five volumes of verse, four with Writers Workshop run by the fabled P. Lal, who provided one of the very few publishing outlets for Indian poets in the early years of Indian independence. He was a teacher of Guha Majumdar in college, and is the subject of one of his poems; and two of his latest books, including the present one, through Silver Bow Publishing, New Westminster, BC CANADA.

The title of the present collection, *Canary Hill,* is explained in an eponymous poem towards the end of the book. Canary Hill is the name of a small, undistinguished hillock near Guha Majumdar's old boarding school where he and his friends would often gather on weekends. The poems of Guha Majumdar are not usually narrative, but several do refer to stories, and all are filled with metaphors and images, a characteristic of the poet's mind which cannot conceive of a person, place, object or event without it bringing a train of associated ideas and sharp, vivid, and sometimes startling or violent images.

Guha Majumdar is a man of many moods, some contrary, even quirky, as is amply evident in his poems. The first volume, *Blunderbuss,* is well titled, for in his verse he shoots off image after image or metaphor after metaphor, seemingly in scatter shot fashion, though they always find their mark and express his meaning. The imagery itself, not just in *Blunderuss* but in all his poems, comes from widely read subject matter and an astonishing variety of sources. Guha Majumdar, besides having been an Associate Professor of English and American literature. specialized also in American drama. He has published several well regarded books in that genre. He is deeply rooted in the language and culture of Bengal, spending his working life in polyglot and culturally diverse Delhi.

He is a singer, a sculptor, an artist. Some of his sketches are included in this book. He is an international traveler who has spent time conducting research at Yale University in the United States. In a tribute to the singer Hemanta Kumar he describes how the singer's soul "every time it left its/walled courtyard willfully lost its way." The reader of Guha Majumdar's poems may well feel the poet has willfully lost his way in the plethora of images that fill his poems, each sharp and vivid but each coming from a vast heterogeneity of sources: the light reflected in the Nainital lake, the guts of a gardener bayonetted in the Bangladesh war, zeppelins, *qawwali* singers, sunrise over the Ganges, men snoring, the maiden of red leaves mentioned in Frederico Garcia Lorca, mountain goats, Ophelia's song as she drowns, the poet Shelley drowning in the Tyrrhenian Sea, Botticelli's Venus, the fingers of a Kathakali dancer... the list could go on and on.

But these images, though they may appear to be piled one on top of another indiscriminately, have a purpose. Take the poem "Faceless Buddha in Bamian," where the wanton destruction of a famous work of art by a Taliban fanatic is described. Through his angry violence the nameless Taliban destroys the human appearance of the Buddha 'til only a faceless, shapeless piece of rock remains. What he does not realize is he has inadvertently revealed the true message of the Buddha, a figure preaching the message of nullity, of nothingness:

> Gone are the lowered eyelids, the downward glance,
> the lucent brow,
> the smile of foreknowledge for
> while possessing the only truth that matters, the truth of
> Nothing as visage; this is what cosmic 'Nothing looks like—

He will never know this or understand, but the ultimate wrecker is also the true, the most profound artist.

Or take a poem that comes late in this collection, "Black Drummer Boy at Harvard Square." On a cold November morning, while people hurry past him without paying him any attention, a cowled black boy is producing music of sorts in Harvard Square by banging away on metal plates, bowls and upturned buckets. A young woman goes past, then returns, takes out a camera and kneels down to get a better shot, but it is not the boy she is photographing but the buildings of Harvard Square. The black boy is invisible to her as to everyone else, as Blacks generally are to White Americans, as Ralph Ellison so brilliantly brought out in his novel. Guha Majumdar could have ended the poem here and it would have been an apt comment on racism in the United States. But tucked away in the poem are another two lines:

I see the black boy's conical parka-hood, an extended shadow of the Doric triangle above the facsimile pillars of Harvard Business School high beyond him. It is given only to the poet to see a vital relationship between the black boy and classical art; indeed, it is given only to the poet to see a genuineness in the black boy compared to the imitation Grecian splendor of the building of the Business School where people learn to make money of the kind the black boy can never even dream of.

It is in these moments of expressing absolute, devastating truths that the true genius of Guha Majumdar shines.

A number of poems are addressed to, or celebrate, the achievements of people whom he admires: Joan of Arc, Henry David Thoreau, Gandhi at Dandi, Srinivas Ramanujan, Eugene O'Neill, Ustad Bismillah Khan. Some celebrate mythical heroes, Durga slaying the demon Mahish-asura, or Bhishma Pitamah and Karna from the *Mahabharata*, Odysseus from Homer. A few deal with works of art, Rodin's *Thinker*, for instance, or seeing Girish Karnad's *Tughlaq* or Tarkovsky's *The Sacrifice*. A couple are devoted to soccer or cricket matches. But the most heartfelt poems are those that deal with the aging and then the death of his mother, or the passing of his father before his time. They are highly restrained, the grief is well controlled but we should not be deluded: the heavy exercise of control is just a device to throw a decent mantle over grief. Take the four-line "Epitaph for My Father," in which he talks about his eyes that saw his father living, then saw him dead, but did not and will not cry. And then his hands, which lit the funeral pyre and will always scald and smolder. There is total restraint here, but also intense pain.

Or take "Reminiscences," where Guha Majumdar reacts after his father has died; and when he sees his father's body,

> I slowly, slowly understood the meaning of 'never,'
> We reached him and held his marble hands ...
> Saw that the large rings on his fingers were missing:
> blood red corals, rubies--blood trickled from his mouth
> upon my sleeves.
> He lay on the ice, heavy, intent, darkening--
> O Lord, O Lord, you tell us so many lies
> to make us sing!

Here, though stated baldly, or rather, because it is stated so baldly the depth of agony at realizing that he will never see his father again is apparent, as is his realization of the hollowness of the consolations that religion offers.

All this is not to suggest that Guha Majumdar is a consistently serious poet. He is capable of rollicking laughter, as becomes apparent in the middle of this volume, where we find an "interlude" of ten limericks. One describes Harry Potter, riding home on an otter, being run over; another Dante who was so well instructed by Virgil that he could not be fooled into believing that a hippopotamus was a tuskless elephant.

But limericks are not Guha Majumdar's forte. He is much more at home in a poem like "Searching for an E-Book" that describes his futile search for Girish Karnad, the dramatist, on Google: he is led on a merry and increasingly frustrating chase by being asked whether he wants information on girl-fish, garish, Grendel-Irish, and then Karma, Karna, Konrad, but is not able to get anything on the subject of his search.

Some of the poems in this volume are ephemeral, but several will live. Rupendra Guha Majumdar's love of the language, the sheer exuberance and joy with which he uses it, the unusual and unexpected connections he draws, his range of reference, the startling and vivid images in these poems, his depth of meaning, will all ensure many of them are read fifty years from now, perhaps by students in the same classrooms of Delhi University where he once taught.

~ Brij Raj Singh

Former Professor of English, Delhi University.
Professor (Emeritus), Hostos Community College
Of the City University of New York.

2024

FOREWORD/ 7
CONTENTS/ 11

I

Bangladesh War and the Cynic's Epilogue / 17
        Illustration/18
Bangladesh War and the Poet's Epilogue / 19
Fugitive / 20
In the Garden / 21
Nocturnal Nainital / 22
Monsoon Spree / 23
Duck Shooting / 23
The Homecoming Soldier / 24
She Saw Above the Blue Hills / 25
Puri by the Sea / 26
Snores / 27
Snatches of a Conversation Overheard in Hell / 28
Poets' Conference / 29
Sonata / 30
Realization / 31
Midnight Vigil / 31
Graffiti of War / 31
Medieval Musings / 32
Song to a Wayward Goddess / 33
Thirst / 34
Temple Street / 35
Femme Fatale at the American Centre library / 36
Formalities / 37
        Illustration/38
Ibex Metamorphosis / 39
Faceless Buddha in Bamian / 40
Afterthought / 41
The Critic's Lecture / 41
On seeing 'Tughlaq' / 42
Apu's Initiation / 45
Vision of the Horse / 48

II

Sunset on the Ganges in Varanasi / 51
Illustration/52
Hungry Stones / 53
Ophelia Downstream / 55
Foreknowledge / 56
David and Goliath: Foregrounding Difference / 57
Assignation in the Durbar / 59
She's Coming / 61
Srinivas Ramanujan / 62
Reminiscences / 64
Epitaph For Father / 67
Madhubani Krishna-Leela / 68
In Considering a Bastille Afternoon / 70
Concern / 72
Campus Encounter / 73
Interlude: Ten 'Limericks': 74-77:
    Taureg Blues / 74
    Transported / 74
    Harry Potter Diary / 74
    Immigration Steps / 75
    Court Wrestler / 75
    Royal Taste / 75
    Captain Hook / 76
    Italian Connection / 76
    Levitational Hazards / 76
    Shakuntala / 77
Accident on the Highway / 78
Kathakali Dancer / 79
Elegy to Karna the Misbegotten / 80
Baul, Street Singer / 82
On Seeing Tarkovosky's film *The Sacrifice* / 83
Library Windows / 85
Memories of a March in Dandi / 86
Baishakh / 87
Antonin Artaud: Eyeless in Thebes / 88
Bheeshma's Sacrifice / 90
Escape from Stalag Luft XVII / 91
Aravali Sunset at Haldighati / 92
New Tenant Catches Up / 92

Illustration/94
Odysseus Preserved / 95
A Tribute to Hemanta Kumar / 96
Yours Irreverently / 97
The Hiroshima Clock / 98
Marriage and Prehistory, Endnotes / 100

III

Train to Motherland / 103
Illustration/104
Durga's Battle / 105
Yale Baby / 107
World Cup Football, 1998: the Goal / 109
Second Baby, At One and a Half / 111
Kargil: War on the Mountains / 112
Metro Suicide / 115
Landscape/ A Scholar's Table / 116
Elegy to a Dove / 117
Pausing at Tao House / 118
Tribute to Ustad Bismillah Khan / 119
In Limbo, Coetzee's *Michael K.* / 120
Searching for an e-Book in the Spring / 121
Surreal Sunset Care of Dali / 123
Rawalpindi Test Match, 2004 / 124
Boys will be Boys / 126
Day of Judgment / 128
Nostos / 129
Cinders / 131
Thoreau's Majority of One / 132
Nocturne: the Buddha Steps Out / 133
Ode to my Fiat Millecento 1100 / 135
Grand Canyon: Notes and Queries / 137
Words Are / 138
Mt. Vesuvius: A Volcano's Legacy / 139
Shelley Descending: Elegy to a Fire Bringer / 140
Landscape with a Peepul Tree by Ramkinkar / 143
Epistle Concerning a Seminal Workshop / 145
Illustration/146
Black Drummer Boy at Harvard Square / 147

Higher Studies / 148
Botticelli's *Birth of Venus* / 148
Uprooted / 149
Aftermath in Kabul 2021 / 150
      Illustration/152
Dolphins in the Time of Corona Lockdown / 153
Gladiator / 154
Pompeii Diary / 155
Telegram from the Outer Circle / 156
To Be a Tiger / 157
Ecology of Sin / 157
Joan of Arc, Endgame / 158
      Illustration/160
Ibex Ram Cares Not For Heights / 161
Dodging / 162
Last Supper / 162
Beauty's Bluff / 162
Final Hearing / 163
Sky High / 163
Adulthood / 163
Rodin's Thinker / 164
Sojourn of the Muse / 165
Canary Hill / 166
Pursuit / 168

Glossary / 169
Bio Data/ 170

I

BANGLADESH WAR AND THE CYNIC'S EPILOGUE

He had heard, so often,
their stories of those
times when
        everything was plentiful and cheap
        and in the evenings
one could repose
beside the Padma and listen
to the songs
        of the fisher folk.

When they said: "You have missed so much!"
he felt uncomfortable and uneasily
shifted his legs and the old doubts returned;
he despised their opulence of memory
where he had no foothold.

On the day he heard about it all,
he shrugged and said; "See! How cheap
are bullets and female chastity,
how deep the songs of vultures
                over the river-bed!"

**Published in *The Illustrated Weekly of India*,
Vol. XCII, #26, June 27(1971), p.22**

Canary Hill – Rupendra Guha Majumdar

BANGLADESH WAR AND THE POET'S EPILOGUE

I have searched many times over
as the candle-flame flickered on the window-sill
fumbling with grimy fingers into the satchel,
searching with ant-haste every corner,
but I could clutch nothing except
a brimming darkness and more dust,
which filled my broken nails.

I have heard laughter in the storm
as I stumbled homewards: it sounded so much
like you that I almost believed it till
the trees shook and blocked my path
with their broken branches.

I have not forgotten your name.
I have not forgotten the way the roof
of my house tilted when they burnt it.
I have not forgotten Bagha's barking
silenced by their bullets
and the cows mooing .

Believe me, I could call them into my power.
I could tell them, "Look, this is not life!"
I could ask them " Have you no shame?
No fear of damnation?"

But I have lost my speech long since
they bayoneted the old gardener,
and the vultures have left his guts
strewn amongst the flowers.

**Published in *The Illustrated Weekly of India*,
Vol. XCII,# 32, August 8(1971), p.15**

FUGITIVE

The footsteps
approached
nearer; in a
reverie of fear
her mind

went back
to the crow
lying dead
on its back on
the cobblestones.

And the ants
came back,
their red
mandibles
clashing

probing into
the privacy
of the bones
of her
      brains.

IN THE GARDEN

Two ink-blue butterflies,
their proboscis curled,
slumber on a Sunflower
like moored yachts
in a quiet harbor
with gaudy sails unfurled.

A great Bumblebee
      goes humming by
like a zeppelin in the sky,
encasing the night
      in each eye.

**Published in *The Illustrated Weekly of India*,
Vol. XCII,#22, May 30 , 1971, p.39**

NOCTURNAL NAINITAL

Rows of overturned
exclamation-marks
of red and white lights
along the lake's edge

form a fence of surprise
holding in the silence
the volcano's secret fear
that spits out dead fish
in the winter.

Arches of weeping-
willows in hushed
whispers, denizens of
the great tremor speak
cajoling me into their
ancient confidence.

A deserted boat drifts
on the moonlit water;
the footfalls of a horse's
clatter is sucked
into the quicksand
of the deep night.

MONSOON SPREE

Hear the storm clouds clap their hands
like *qawwali* singers, waiting for the downpour
                    of applause.

**(Published in *The Illustrated Weekly of India*,
Vol. XCII,# 52, December 26 (1971), p.47)**

DUCK-SHOOTING

Like a frog-tongue
the barrel-fire flicked, fell
   from
        the air
          the bird,
the sudden break
in the arrowhead
        of geese.

Somewhere
    crumpled, unstrung,
a bouquet of feathers
settled amongst the reeds,
    unsung.

**Published in *The Miscellany*,
Nov-Dec 1970,No. 42,p.8**

THE HOMECOMING SOLDIER

Lad, you seek the direction? First, turn
left, you will see in front of you masts,

barrels, riggings, unmended nets,
tattooed sailors smoking cigars,

girls walking quickly past diners,
lodgings, bars, a few teashops;

walk on along the dock, in the wind
you will get the hot smell of chops.

Then take the second right turn;
a small red cottage with shutters closed,

an untended garden basking in the sun
beyond a wide gate you will see—it's

a house poised beside an old Neem tree,
one unlatched window banging in the wind.

I think that is the house you are looking for—
the house where your mother died.

SHE SAW ABOVE THE BLUE HILLS

She saw above the blue hills
prolific clouds pressed
together like those overfed
cherubim of Peter Paul Rubens.

Footfalls in the deep forest
crackled on dry twigs, acorns
and leaves; she waited for him,
smiling in abeyance.

She knew he would come
stumbling through the bushes;

and she twined strands of
night-hair around her fingers,
        smiling.

PURI BY THE SEA

I heard during
the moonless nights
the restless waves resounding
like a bull moose bellowing
in mating season.

The sea-shells
on the whipped sands
looked like chipped fingernails
of desperate hands.

Crabs scurried along
the deserted beach.
They too had destinations
                    to reach.

SNORES

Squads of snores
skiing down mucus

slopes excitedly
grumble
outrageously

as they tumble in
bewildered heaps

into the clutches
of bushy mustaches.

SNATCHES OF A CONVERSATION OVERHEARD IN HELL

"I have a house in Atlantis, fully furnished
With foibles of fantastic fashions...
Now its inhabitants are fish."

"I think I left my radio on in my Alpine shack
Last summer when I died: I wonder for
How many days the news fell down
The mountain side... perhaps,
The goats tried the taste of jazz!"

"There was so much to think of... so much
To think of."

**Published in *Indo-English Poetry in Bengal*,
Translated into Bengali & Edited by K.C. Lahiri/
Calcutta: Writers Workshop, 1974**

POETS' CONFERENCE

The poets
smiled

        at each other,
          whittling away
at twigs
of infinities.

"Stitches
       take time
        my friends,

take time
to heal!"

SONATA

How much longer could we
have lived in that tepid silence
of poses, you and I molding
the soft new sky with our fingers
and lacing the night with marigolds
                and roses ?

Perhaps, you can tell me why
my mind leapt out of its meshes
of mist, scattering memories in its wake
like seeds to sprout and stand and twist
in the wind's way and fade to ashes
            with the lightning's kiss.

Perhaps, no longer is it all
an awkward entrancement of joys
that must crumble and fall around
our fecund hopes, like toys.

Perhaps, we know each other now.

REALIZATION

They said
It would be a verdure sight,
And so with conceptions
Of seraphic forms in infancy
I went to see.

They said
They had forgotten the genre
Of truth to fill from
Mythic streams; and so with a jar
Of commodious size
I went to seize.

I saw all,
Even tamed a few who came
to kill; but returning, at the gate
I fell and from the broken jar
All truth did spill.

MIDNIGHT VIGIL

Upstairs, the faint tiny tinkle of glass,
their laughter slips down the teak banisters.

"Patience, patience...." purrs the cat,
observing keenly my nervous eyes.

GRAFFITI OF WAR

On his withered face a tilted smile appears,
flits through the ashes of nine brave sons.

MEDIEVAL MUSINGS

With a seeming mission
some low dog howleth
in the moon-choked scrub;

now born newly
    and well
is your brown bored owl
of suspicion :
           rheumatic,
unblinking,
        still.

SONG TO A WAYWARD GODDESS
a tribute to the Andalusian poet, Federico Garcia Lorca

1

I met her then, the Queen of Seasons,
in the forest beside the Mad River;
her eyes were dark prehistoric swamps,
her large hips bloody in the wake of thorns.

I know the forests here and the streams
and the burrows of the sly vixens
and each rock that warms the reptile's belly
and the quicksands born of old curses.

I called her by name—Maiden of the Red Leaves—
and she came to me with the pride of rivers,
her black hair swirling like quick, untamed eddies,
her breasts unplucked cool lotus buds at dawn.

2

Words grappled like urchins in the alleys of my voice;
words crumpled like deer with sudden arrows in their
      throats;
words rose like the ashes of the temples that smoldered
      in the heart of the exiled king;
words became birds blinded by hail and crashed like stones
      through the branches of trees;
words became leaves, red, red leaves,
      ripe Maiden of the Red Leaves.

I know the forests here and the streams
and the paths that lead to the caves of the weary
and the great cliffs that soar above somnolent brows
and the heartbeats of the invisible in the mists of silence.

3

And through the dim forest came the Mad River :
the waves were wild stallions rushing down the mountains,
    hooves of bronze, manes of foam;
the waves were wounded boars plunging at the hunter,
    curved tusks of silver, blue skins of ice;
the waves were anacondas with tails on fire,
    tongues of whirlpools, eyes of lost shadows.

Let me wipe the blood from your hips,
        Maiden of the Red Leaves!
Come, we shall bathe in the foam of the Mad River!
The thorns of this forest are long and painful,
    but you did not know it,
        being the Queen of Seasons.

THIRST

Night comes over the desolate land,
        smelling of rain, proud.
The moon, an impatient calf,
        plucks at the full udders of a cloud.

TEMPLE STREET, NEW HAVEN
Along Temple Street beside the central Green square in New Haven, Connecticut, stand three churches in a row, founded during Puritan times of the first settlers in the 17th century.

All these years upright,
*three hou*ses of God
elbow to elbow on the Green,
is a bit too much,

since it was
pilgrims who were
supposed to converge there,
not walls of stone
turned eastwards
to give thanks for
small mercies rendered.

But watch!
At dusk, the three towers
become the blunted trident
of the bronzed sea-god*
poised for recompense
for all the children who did not reach
this Green square of grass
downtown to feed the pigeons,

their small hands
still push the wracked waves
onwards, their breaths
                        lift gently
the seagulls
           over the foam.

---

*Poseidon

FEMME FATALE AT THE
AMERICAN-CENTRE LIBRARY

She sat opposite me, exquisitely,
she was a rare one of nature's whips,
she had on a thick pink shawl
and soft open matching lips.

It was a brief mid-day pause in a sleek
panther's prowl; beside her all,
all fair was foul.

And the other men looked furtively past
my brash, bristly chin; but the fleas
of their pale eager glances could hardly
bother her priceless skin — she flicked
them off with the tail of her brisk composure!

Behind me loomed nimbus, a loud
          'SILENCE PLEASE!'
Yet boldly did I ask her,
      my vision's antennae aquiver,
could you spare me a sheet of paper, Miss?

She nodded, smiled and gave me *two*!
Like a fool I wrote this poem then,
did not catch her hint--
              did nothing do!

FORMALITIES

She apologized for the old table-fan
making so much of a noise,
a family heirloom, quite *cute* otherwise.

He apologized for having kissed her
without permission, coughed uneasily,
praised the *elichi* flavour of the tea.

Canary Hill – Rupendra Guha Majumdar

IBEX METAMORPHOSIS

IBEX METAMORPHOSIS

In Ovid's '*Metamorphoses*' after Polyphemus the Cyclops, out of sheer jealousy, kills Acis the lover of the sea-nymph Galatea, she prays to her divine father Nereus, to transform her deceased mortal lover into a river so she could be united with him forever.

The problem of walking demurely along this two-inch shelf is
it's across a perpendicular cliff-face soaring into clouds
hundreds of feet above ground zero in the Hindu Kush.

Yet, this *blanche*, nimble pair of Ibex prospecting rock-salt
and moss in every nook and cranny with tongue-tips quivering,
no dread of a slip up of hooves, a sudden hurtling down
the wall of sheer indifference,

knowing in the extra twinkle in their eyes, far from home,
Amun their ram-headed god of Kush and kin will break their fall
on any glistening boulder so far below, switch them — curving
horns and fleece and bones—
                       into cascading water,
                  white
                          blossoming foam.

FACELESS BUDDHA IN BAMIAN

This Gandhara statue on the rocky outskirts
of Bamian has no face to speak of
in present tense — no eyes, nose, ears, lips
that form the lineaments we can recognize
from Mauryan art and meditation, all wiped clean
        with angry blows of a redoubtable hammer.

Gone are the lowered eyelids,
the downward glance, the lucent brow,
the smile of foreknowledge for the
while possessing the only truth that
matters, the truth of Nothing as visage;
this is what cosmic 'Nothing' looks like —

a face that once was, redundant now;
the man who did this, the man with
the demented hammer is nowhere
around to marvel at his own meticulous
handiwork: the censure of unwanted gods,
incising the gamut of senses —
        sight, smell, hearing, speech —

the outcome that Gautama surely wants
when he pauses on the threshold of time
and sees another dawn bleed softly into the valley.
The hammer-man perspires under the sun,
his shoulders ache in labor as his arms
swing back and forth in rapt exhaustion, strike

away the sand-stone enraptured eyes, nose,
ears, lips, chin -- the repertoire of senses from
the face of the earth; the man with the hammer,
dispenser of all unwanted faces unduly gazing
from horizon to horizon, one life to another --

    he comes as a blessing, redeems
    the dispensable mask of the last saviour

.

AFTERTHOUGHT

Her mind's patched, wrinkled, sails now arch steady, proud,
peacock breasted, bewitching the brusque horizon numb.

Now unchained from his droll, dungeon-laughter, she sits
for long hours on the veranda by herself and shadow; repeats

the caged restless parrot: "What was he actually after?"

But hate wilted since he left
				an unsigned letter,
						in longhand, under the door,
								since
										he left

THE CRITIC'S LECTURE

After his staccato stammers
And amphibious enunciation
And some loss of memory
And wild wind-mill gestures,

The inadequate applause made matters worse.

'I wonder *what* they consider fit', he cursed!
Then he took out his handkerchief
		and sneezed into it!

ON SEEING *TUGHLAQ* AT THE PURANA-QILA THEATRE

Girish Karnad's play *Tughlaq* (I saw with a friend) portrays the life of the medieval "mad" king Muhammad-bin-Tughlaq who compelled his subjects to migrate from Delhi to his new capital in Daulatabad, a thousand miles away in central India.

1

The mob is there before him, the king,
flourishing with utter choric ease
their cheap trinkets of intrigue.
It is mentioned in the bold red brochure
that the company has taken, on loan, each beard and wig.

Tughlaq enters in blazing yellow holding
a scimitar before him with both hands shoulder-high,
the Machiavellian. Higher up, there's lightning
in each eye.
        Many shrivel.

Like all strategic kings, Tughlaq plays chess:
he makes a move: from Delhi to Daulatabad, stings
his slow-footed assassins-to-be in prayer.
You too, Shihabuddin? You too? You?
The knife punctuates the question marks
        through the prince.

2

In the night of Daulatabad he hears the jackals laugh.
In the market place his step–mother lies under a heap
of stones; her body hangs wilted at the stake;
he could grant her no other death.
In the night of Daulatabad, the crouching jackals laugh.
In the night of Daulatabad, he hears the hag,
        the deserted city, beckon.

"Tughlaq the lonely!
        The immaculate butcher!

> The darkling unfathomed!
> The misunderstood fox!
> The unabated bull!
> Return to me!

Tughlaq the lonely and all the loud winds against you
and your footsteps echo with lessening dread
along the corridors of bleached white bones.

Who will bide, Tughlaq?
> On the ramparts the new recruit
> cannot grasp the tide of your words.
> You fling him over the roof wall into space!

Who will bide Tughlaq?
You clutch a dream born amongst the breath of corpses.
Hear the neighing of your shackled horses!
> Return to me!

The blood-stains have dried, all of them, like red chillies
> in the sun,

the blood of your brother, of Shihabuddin,
the blood of the high priest and of your father;
the blood on the cobbled streets
> and in the undiscovered vaults;

the blood that no one saw, glimmering beyond
cloistered shadows, but still whispering;
the blood of your many sacrifices, whipped
> and shivering;

the blood that I drank and swayed under;
the blood that revived me, four years ago.

Now there is only dust and weeds and more dust
and the bald circling crows clamouring and the low
moaning of ghosts in the bleak evenings;
> Return to me!

I have become worn and pale, my countenance
devoid of your sword's hot blood, my undug graves
so starved of meat. Return to me!
Again bathe me with your own hands Tughlaq!

The bejeweled *twaif* Delhi beckons;
and from the clouds up high circling vultures croak
> "Tughlaq! Tughlaq!

3

His mind soars above the tourist-ruins,
fitted so cleverly with stage-lights, which
felicitously reveal him in strategic plights
between hoary hell and heaven.

Aakash, sitting attentively on my right, suddenly
declares about the tickets: "We should have
bought the seats in the rear, not these in front.
We are too close." Precipitously I reply, "It's hot!"

The lights dim low.
Tughlaq, in black and gold trimmings, sits on
top of the stone stairs, tired, without any attendants
or drink or background music.

All around, slow shadows cluster trapping cobwebs
and spider and ancient rock.
A bat sweeps out of the broken arches
like a splinter of shadow snatched up by the wind.

All around the foul, nascent embers, squeezed dry
of smoke but still smoldering, blinding the sky,
forever groping.

Stranger that you are, no less, stranger that you'll be —
move far from this glorious ruin
    and seek no more this aching darkness.

A high billow of dust sprouts along the prodigal trail.
    The horizon blinks.

Across the Jamuna, crouching,
              storm-clouds growl:
                          "Tughlaq! Tughlaq!"

**(Published in *Vagartha*,
ed. Meenakshi Mukherjee, July 1975, No.10, , p.16-19)**

APU'S INITIATION

**The overt delay of little Apu to speak as a normal child
evoked immense tension at multiple levels of reality and
prenatal imagination... 'til the right moment was duly reached.**
**

> "The child is searching for his voice
> (The king of the crickets had it)
> In a drop of water the child was searching for his voice."
> — Federico Garcia Lorca

1

Apu yawned, yawned,
too new in sleep to choose his dreams,
he paused on the brink of the *bhikkhus'*
path, one-vision old, told the apsaras
to resume their dance;
he knew the deep demanding wait,
the wild unwillowy, unbending years,
           but he would not be late,
             he knew.

Ah! Though great king he was earlier,
well, say in the Mauryan times and now
court and kind lay fossil-carved, close,
lime-cluttered, could he blend with winds
that were dream-starved like fraught stallions
rearing wildly, teeth bared and glistening...
           but caught.

    "Apu, try the pale purple flowers
on the scrub beside the great waterfall; its
name dances — Dhatura, Shiva's;
       go, drink its poison, fortunate
if you are... the blue-throated death
               will be yours.

O Manu! Will not your flames dance in the emerald cave?

2

"Speak, speak! Come Apu! Talk your fill!
Say more than Ma, say... say the needful,
more than needful, truth or lie, throw it on us,
but TALK! Say the cat is coming, the dog is
mewing, the bird is coughing, the cow is
hissing; say moooo; be it 'bat' or 'rat', but
speak! Say 'a' for mud and blood
is gold, but speak!   Apu?"

But Apu lay benign in bed, dumb, wide-eyed,
curled, pretending a penultimate death, tired
with the well-wishes upon him heaped, big
groaning blessings and kisses of grannies
and nannies; lucky he forgot his Mauryan reign —
"Notions of grandeur!" declared the winds,
perhaps, gave him pain.

O Manu! When will your flames dance in the emerald cave?

Wanton lies the tongue in silence,
wanton the eyes that cannot defy the fingers
beckoning towards the soft bed of leaves, her
delicious shadow.

  Come out of your shell, traitor turtle, beak
        bent, blinking! Why are you withering
           in this untimely hour?

3

Through the bleak bamboo forest the Sun
creaked down, touched tentatively the puffed
pond slime, bloomed slowly into a lotus shyly.
The poison intruded late; but then the elfin
time stood steady like an upright stork stuffed.

Snaking, the sudden lightning split the shackled
untaught night, entered his third eye as he slept
soundly, shook the ventricles and valves vastly,
the needles trembled without shame; swept
the heaving, hoary laughter through the graphs!

O yes, yes! Even the close corpuscles growled,
"Give us this day our daily bread!"

Ah! The blue trembling stream rushed
shimmering up the spine, spiraled screaming up
the centuries like a betrayed eagle up
the centuries for Bindusara and all to the tongue
took the test!

Yielded the somnolent, gilded dream and Apu spoke!
    O little Apu spoke!

O Manu! Manu! Your flames are now dancing
                              in the emerald cave!

VISION OF THE HORSE

Smelling spring whiffs
of freedom before
         the moon,

the sand-white stallion rears
its head, stamps twice.

The boulder's crest
Shakes from its mane

the last dread
whispers
         of the wind.

II

SUNSET ON THE GANGES IN VARANASI

1

The river swallows quickly, with little sound:
stiff, reeling bodies of beggars mainly, unlabeled bottles,
brass goddesses, frail temptations of dim lit rooms;
the wind that will not restrain its wagging tongue
        divulges the subtle trails of ancient tortoises.

But for a change, a dead saint passes, amazed
(while serenely floating) at what passes for time,
amazed truly at the briskness of things that heave
and squander in moments of scorn, his eyebrows
raised in permanent wonder, his eyes recall
        the familiar implacental shore.

Irresolute bubbles, braided ripples, marigolds of torn
garlands gather the tremors of last unspoken words;
crows caw, priest-like, before subdued, weary minstrels
        who know all but one shrill song.

2

What soft vermillioned feet ascend the wet stone steps
and walk briskly past the shadows of huddled wailing forms?
What last measured prayer at dawn will undo the heavy locks
        of divine slumber
and drive the rampant locusts of ageless memories
past the studded gates of burning cities ?

The wind with the twisted ankle
        moans amidst the cool rice fields.
    The whirlpools dance like delirious witches.

3

    One stray, bobbing marigold wanders
    recklessly to the horizon   and stumbles.

Becoming Sun,
        it too is swallowed, quickly,
                with little sound.

HUNGRY STONES

HUNGRY STONES

A short story, "Khudito Pashan" (*Hungry Stones*) by Rabindranath Tagore draws on a man's memories of a previous life connected to an exotic palace

These are familiar
ruins said the young
man hands in pockets
small eyes narrowed
hair tousled by the
wind

      footsteps echo
down the stone corridors
past fat crouching
gargoyles and blanched
Aphrodites standing
demurely around
the shattered fountain

strange
      said the young
graduate as the sky
darkened and more
footsteps echoed down
the stone corridors

      the remorseless
shuffling gait of
hunched phlegmatic
priests the measured
tread of scheming
ministers whispering

      behind the
buttressed pillars how
long had their knives
been rusting in their
scabbards

the rain washes the
bare sprawling floor
of the great hall
through the green
broken glass of the
casements the rice
fields can be seen for
miles clutching
burnt out firebrands
of trees

I have a vivid
imagination said he
and laughed climbing the
wide curving staircase
towards the open
      bejeweled arms
of his smiling
   exquisite
          princess

OPHELIA DOWNSTREAM
A twilight drowning in a brook in Denmark

At the bend of winter's
dark forest flittered her
silken face in a brook still
quivering with expectations,
death.

Some righteous song
splashes amongst the reeds
and sinks through the flurry
of circling minnows,

simmers through imperfect,
inundated memory, unmindful,
unmitigated, surprisingly resolute,
    silken,
            glittering.

FOREKNOWLEDGE

What follows from you
an entire summer afternoon
speckled and brief
        stark without
a trace of future moment in
the span of old prerequisites
and fame;
       what explodes in
the trail of sleek flying-fish,
pushes boulders over pinnacles

of shame upon my small square
cluttered table
        at the corner –

  consider now

       and maybe,
laughing, eyes closed or merry,
reclaimed in dream, memory
      and song,
a member
    of this dusk's
      congregation that
holds its fort with cold
foreboding —

    you sleep with
premonitions beside me, your
dark brown body so strangely
quivering, quite unknown
    to lesser
        evil.

DAVID AND GOLIATH: FOREGROUNDING DIFFERENCE

"Let no one lose heart on account of this Philistine."
(David, *Samuel: 32*)

1

I will fight you, he cried
                      and picked up a stone.
I will fight you, he said
                      as he peered into those eyes.
I will fight you he thought
                      touching the tousled
desert wind
          on his hair.

Closing in on the stretch of no-man's-land,
girded with giant cacti on slopes and sharp cries
of circling kestrels, big and small meet
                      at the level of ground zero

before a bolt of sharp lightning-licked sling-stone
cracks the wrinkled firmament
                      of a behemoth's brow
     right
          at the epicenter.

2

Goliath sinks heavily in a cloud of dust biting
his own tongue of untested fear, his eyes roll
in the thick blood of his sockets, the champion
More-than-Man crashes in heavy armour
clanging to the earth, an overshadowing, gross,
over-the-top Philistine chokes on the ignominy
          of brute fangled words.

The immediate lowliness of earth serves
the pressing purpose of the unlettered,
unseasoned lad calling a spade a spade
          knowing that customized armour
or helmet only pulls a big, blunted body down,

does not protect in battle — oversized shield,
    ornate studded wrath

       of a gilded grimacing Medusa-visage
                  of no real worth.

The scimitar loosened from the big man's grasp
serves Dave's immediate purpose
           of a neat *coup de grace* to
separate head from neck
at the crucial turn of the spine,
    a fountain spouts, congeals
          into the rarest of desert flowers.

3

Your young boy-shepherd counting his sheep
before the sun sets in the ravines -- he does
the honours, patriarch-to-be of the clan, no big deal,
once chastising stray lions or their snarling shadows
       in the tall elephant-grass.

But here he raises high the disjointed trophy by the hair
against fleeting parturient clouds dripping a trail
       of purple blossoms.

Blood is real, thick, and glistening,
    this fountain spring of darkening blood
                    spouting for ages.

ASSIGNATION IN THE DURBAR

1

Such perfection sought for
in the small hours of a terse
windy new-year midnight,
so compromisingly deep cluttered
that not even the bells are
ringing in advance of our resolutions.

Laughter is there, drinks
aplenty, the flutter of ancient
ribaldry between thin trembling
jeweled fingers, benign transience —

but must you move so
quickly from this glittering room
into your evening of uncertain quibbles,
you who spoke, you who came to me,
you who vouched to bear my child
and lead it beyond
        the clutches of evil ?

2

See memory through this
        marble screen: here pain
may not enter beyond the eunuch's
sword, the flash of the cobra's
tongue, nurtured over the years
within walls where women and music
        ripened together.

Late in the night...
        late in the night,
the opium rhythm of dancing feet
gliding over black silken marble
to the brink of his resplendent bed.

He watches her few moments of quiet
disrobing in the glimmer of fire;
smiling, she unclasps her last button
of diamond, unties her black ropes
of hair, touches his perspiring
forehead with her long fingers;
she has seen him, she says,
in a childhood dream
where sky and sea
crumbled into birds

    and god laughed over
      his mellow wine.

Brisk is the tumult of timely
recognition beyond the fullness of
drunken speech, abounding fears —

the moon crushed under the hooves
of stampeding clouds, the moon split
like a reluctant oyster, stiffens
          against
                the mountain.

SHE'S COMING
to e. e. cummings

break
     the funny
    clutch the
oof! malicious

but there
    she comes full
vanity galore well
balancing on the acute
bridge of
    her Hellenic
nose a gold frosted nose
pince-nez

    now don't
grumble if I'm
ambitious

       click

SRINIVAS RAMANUJAN

Mathematician extraordinaire

A taut fabric sky ripped by
lightning, shredded into small
dark bits of cloud and
scattered;
        thunder declares the
birth of a true genius lately
citizen of another planet in
another distant galactic deep.

Dry tamarind leaves swirl in
whirlpools around his rocking
cradle, brass bells tinkling;
a light shimmers over the faded
blue muslin that grandmother
presented, smiling to herself
for the way things were going.

His father keeps accounts in
the cloth-shop in Kumbakonam
and can spell Orthodoxy
        backwards.

In school he stares wide-eyed
at the dark limpid beauty of
mathematics, in awe bows low
and delves into equations
beyond the square-roots of penury.

Now, wearing a gray baggy coat,
he has no time to shave or to fuss
over his English which is
preposterous.

        His forte
is Numbers, its great fun; unlike
you or me or Pope Leo or Gregory

he quite easily measures Infinity.
He tells me, with a wink,
all adds up to One, not Zero !
It's great fun
            for our hero !

He will die early, at the age of
thirty-three, scribbling a theorem
on the cluttered table, rice and
boiled potatoes untouched,
salt-cellar clown overturned,
the cat clawing at the door
'til the end of evening.

The storm recedes over the palm trees.
The thunder sleeps in the valley.

REMINISCENCES

Fragments from a family's collective unconscious

1

The mud of my ancestors clings
on the wall there, splattered like
many burnt starfish flung up
on an evening that melted in
the sea's bowels.

Grandfather's words in messages
of dark recondite blood smudge
the blade of his sword though jammed
within the velvet scabbard arched
over his favourite cupboard now
throbbing with a heart of clock.

In the photograph all is told, even
the strange resemblance with me, aunt said,
the mustache curling the opposite way,
        however.

2

In the greenhouse a cat mews beyond
a preponderance of dung, knocking
brusquely a low Scarabaeus beetle
into a bucket which had catered to
        rhododendrons and ferns.

The wasps sway in the air like abandoned
flowers thrown into turbulent gutters;
upon the table a great bull caterpillar
swaggers boldly through the moss, drawn
by mirages of dark rose petals;
the floor gleams with large scattered
alphabets of glass reflecting the traffic
of garrulous sparrows; spiders peel leprous
skins of plaster, mouthing frantic syllables
of flies in the vortex of their webs.

3

These are the holy men with shaven
heads and poignant downward glance;
they enter the narrow garden path at dusk
when none can see their shadowed faces;
they climb the hollow stairs and begin
their songs:

they come through the cold night
and will not conspire to laugh ever
for they know the bleak, demented howl
of the valley foxes.

The bell tolls in the forest-temple.
The river claws our young sandy shores.

4

Grandfather, lawyer, adept with sword
and stave, often sparred with his criminal
clients, invoking the spirit of Raja
Pratapaditya as his incandescent birthright,
a scion of Surya, of the house of Ikshvaku.

At seventy, one sultry afternoon, he speared
a jackal scrambling past the pond with his
favourite milk-white hen; at eighty he got
worried for the first time, historically
speaking, and speculating upon the ingratitude

of memory, chronicled conscious *Khatriya*
genesis in virile rhetoric: erstwhile
ancestors, belligerent progeny, evidence and
imagination — rubbed shoulders for one
impeccable rupee as the price.

He crossed ninety with an iron grip that
would not submit to death 'til death pushed
his hand down slowly upon the table, both
grunting with pride, both exhausted finally.

Grandmother was a genius with mango
and other pickles; she loved gossiping with
all the neighboring housewives in their respective
households in the time it took for the rice to
soften over the ebbing coal fire.

At seventy-five she turned almost mad.
muttering to herself the names of her
eleven children and her two dead sons-in-law,
one crushed by a peremptory truck,
the other poisoned by government officials.

5

Father died at sixty-two, lonely,
as he had always prophesied,
looking more dignified than ever;

I slowly, slowly understood the meaning of 'never'.
We reached him and held his marble hands,
saw that the large rings on his fingers were missing:
blood-red corals, rubies –
                    blood trickled from his mouth
              upon my sleeves.

He lay on the ice heavy, intent, darkening;

O Lord, O Lord! you tell us so many lies
                                 to make us sing.

EPITAPH FOR FATHER

These are my eyes that saw you living.
These are my eyes that neither cried nor will.
These are my hands that set you aflame.
These are my hands that are smoldering still.

MADHUBANI KRISHNA-LEELA
The eastern Indian folk-art of Madhubani colorfully evokes many mythic narratives with flair.

The tree is his hand, trellised with the ochre
paste of thick turmeric and the pubescent
vermilion, splayed skywards, simmering;
Orange flowers blossom from sudden fingertips
of curving branches.

The dark blue sky, flaunting its doves, is
smothered by the leaves of the Jacaranda;
and ropes of clouds trip the seething monster
on the dust before His small dancing feet.

Radha reconsiders the evening's schedule
at a critical moment surpassing silence, smiling
at the wantonness of two inspired peacocks
on the brink of the brimming river at Gokul.

He postpones the storm, caressing a calf, moves
three paces into the green bounds of home;
the wind blows past man's ancient fears,
the wind bows to His eternal flute.

Lotus nudes, coy Gopis in the pond, pink with
affected shame, arms raised to the branches where
He knows what follows the smell of rain;
petticoats with waves of gold and a galaxy

of strategic tinsel, blouses that enhance
the firm breasts of nimble virgins, He showers
amidst them in the end.

Beholding his wonder
          is a full-time occupation :
and these women here know it though they have
husbands. The word "though" is quaint conjunction.

After the daily chores
and all asleep, utensils scrubbed and lanterns

dimmed, doors creak open
with the help of the wind....

Moonlight beckons a pretty assembly.

Radha is in the thick of the game.

IN CONSIDERING A BASTILLE AFTERNOON

1

The days being serialized regarding
knowledge, one portion of fact following
upon the heels of another, sometimes uninvited
guests indifferent to scorn, or a poor relative
convalescing;

The unexpected moment in facile history
then stiffens, silencing the fearful heart
and departs quietly through the back-yard, past
the scattered tin cans and tyres and black
arching tomcats, as if nothing had happened in
the vicinity of the stubbed cigarette.
        Nothing worth mentioning for instant
    resolution.

Knowledge flounders on the cobbled
alleys of the market-place, twisted in
fury, demented, frothing, spitting out
                      a revolution.

2

Pulled up the thirty-foot wooden frame
by crazed fingers, the heavy blade

glistens sanguine in the sun and ponders,
crashes to a halt where the Neck ended
and the Voice began
                with a little effort.

The heads gather in the basket like soiled
              cabbages;
the heads belong to no one in particular now;
the heads would now surely
        reconsider the nativity of passions.

The basket says, enough. There is no more
space to keep them, except on the points
         of your long-exhausted spears.

The river is as bloody as your hands.
The sky is dark
                with your dangerous memory.

CONCERN

Keeping you intact in
my shell of care
                then
warding off the bees with

all their stings and stripes
and much besides —

what time will I give to the
confluence of streams
that smother with a rush?

What moment will I dream
for the salvation of my gods?

what pilgrimage gather into
the folds of my death?

CAMPUS ENCOUNTER

Engine still thudding
                      we parked
Outside the hostel wall to talk a while
The time being ten past nine pm still
An hour to go

The road was deserted but for
Occasional streaks of cars one swung
Towards ours be careful you said

White ambassador with six or seven
Of them peering like jackals in
The forest screeched
                      to a halt beside
My door to halt with quite obvious
Intent

Though old and whimsical my car
in a trice sprang like a black panther
out of their closing grasp
                      with a roar

reaching destination around the corner
hop off I told you engine thudding ages
it took for the iron
                      gates to open
and engulf you safely

tomorrow you leave for home alone
air-conditioned coach all the way nose
pricked and sore
                      remember the furious
graph of our presumptuous
          knowing

INTERLUDE: TEN 'LIMERICKS'

TAUREG BLUES

There was a Taureg warrior from Timbuktu
who like all his tribe imbibed the complexion blue
from the thick indigo robes he wore throughout the year;

but on New Year's Day he swore, enough
was enough! He would opt at once
                        for some other hue!

TRANSPORTED

Harry, a West-Indian driver of a London double-decker
Chortled tunes from songs of the late Chubby Checker!

The beats, of course, recalled the irrepressible 'Twist'!
But the road ahead being totally engulfed in mist,

The commuters all prayed for their lives to their Maker!

HARRY POTTER DIARY

There was this whiz kid by the name of Potter
Who would often ride back home on an otter!

Perchance he slipped into the fast lane one day!
The traffic police were quite perplexed
                        but had not a *thing* to say!

After all, he was a mighty best seller
                      and not a stupid rotter!

IMMIGRATION STEPS

Once a rare ass from the Great Rann of Kutch*
Met a migratory pink flamingo who was *just* a little
                                               out of touch

With the basic steps of the dance Lambada — no, not
Flamenco! — that just by chance happened to be

The visa qualifier at the local embassy of the Dutch!

COURT WRESTLER

A wrestler in the erstwhile Court of Travancore
At the end of each bout let out a stupendous roar,

Like a lion bursting out of a smug trapper's net—
O! It was a cry you could hardly ever forget!

And his *chelas* would instantly applaud, "Encore, encore!"

_____

ROYAL TASTE

The French poodle of Prince Salman Ali Jung
Had an odd penchant for the local concoction *bhaang*!

When asked about her lowly taste in wines,
They said it was an indulgence only on those days

She played Frisbee with the Prince—
                    With the Frisbees all made of dung!

CAPTAIN HOOK

An adventurer by the name of Conway
Lived in a bunker beside a civilian runway.

With a long bamboo-pole and a hook
He quit playing by the book,

Latching on to planes to Mongolia and back—
              The Hun-way!

ITALIAN CONNECTION

We recall the medieval poet Alighieri Dante
Who lived in Florence, took nothing for granted

With ancient Virgil as mentor and guide
Really none could take him for an extended ride—

Like, passing off a hippopotamus for a toothless
                            elephanté !

LEVITATIONAL HAZARDS

Once there was a certain NRI lady from Poona
Who claimed she could levitate much soona

Than all those obfuscating TM*-*wallas*
Who held such workshops in downtown Dallas.

So she waved "Bye bye" to her friends sweetly,
Drank a large glass of *nimbu-pani*, belched discreetly,

Changed gears.... but alas... fell in a swoona !

(^TM: Transcendental Meditation)

SHAKUNTALA

A young king, out hunting incognito, falls in love with and marries a forest maiden, Shakuntala; he returns home after promising her a formal welcome to his kingdom. However, he dishonors his own promise after losing his memory

---

She was a forest maiden, her name, Miss Shakuntala
Who got tied up with His Highness of Kapurtala;

But later when she presented him with their child,
He had quite forgotten her and turned wild,

Exclaiming, "What nonsense! He's not *my* Nandalala!"

ACCIDENT ON THE HIGHWAY

Even for a second, Monsieur, you cannot afford
to doze off while at the wheel of your car down
Mathura or any other road at 60mph, wife sitting
next to you; daughter dozing too, curled up on
the back seat dreaming of scaling sundry peaks in
               the Garhwal ranges.

Two spurts of dozing create a third, as they
say, it's inevitable — in the infectious dozing mode
the car turns turtle on hitting a wayside rock, skids
screeching long three hundred yards in a shattering
pile of steel and glass then stops against a tree!

Mercifully, girl, you were dozing and not sticking
your neck and head out of the window like smiling
dogs do to lap up the breeze;
                        for, then, with the car
crashing on its side your head would have
rolled off down the meadows like a free-wheeling
ripe melon dislodged from the master's cart
            to merge with fleeting shadows.

The blood that was gushing from your left temple
          is stanched in the ICU
with care and three and forty stitches now
undone, dried
and shining like stray silvery sea-shells
                   on sun-kissed beaches .

Dozing is an act you learn inside the womb--
it is the first lesson of a newfound birth
         you have earned on the blazing highway
         in telling or listening to stories
         without pain or fear
     of the deep secrets
           of passage
                  and the tomb!

KATHAKALI DANCER

In one palm
        upwards
you cup the world
like a tiny wet bird
watch it
        and reconsider
its blue green plumage
shimmer
        from every angle

In the other
        smiling
you place the sky
curving it deftly with
your arched fingers
        rounding the far
edges so that all
the known winds return
where they started from

to help a speckled blue
green bird
wings dried and ready
glide tirelessly back to
where it started from

across the trackless
midnight oceans of your
eyes
    beyond the mediating
echoes of your dancing
        feet

ELEGY TO KARNA, THE MISBEGOTTEN

1

During this loud millennial war
our supple prayers are muted; they soon subside
and stiffen, taking the shape of rough red mounds
of earth unskinned of grass, raw, clenched knuckles
of earth's midwinter hands freezing upon
      Death's throat without
              a further scuffle.

Karna's dead, subjected to the late
vulnerability of all semi-divine heroes
who have the indulgences of their mothers
and the curses of irascible sages to account for
      in their penultimate hours.

Kunti's firstborn, first to know exile
from urban assurances; since birth the Outsider,
sold to the river, biding his time, lurking
behind trees measuring the pure pulse of war
beyond his family's hearth:
         when despair came
    he swallowed his spittle.

2

At the inception of the prologue, Nature
plays truant with the hero, unnerving the formal
conditions of his birth, eschewing promises, yet
holding back the keen fangs of the evening wolf
from his basket beside the riverbank.
Nature dispenses with his immediate royal ties
in a huff
     to engender in him the role
of a deeper passion;
             dispenses with his
righteous claims to superior instruction
     to engender in him the pain
of becoming the perfect archer;

                         dispenses with
his godly armour
                    that he may be redeemed in death
     more quickly
     at the hands of his rival,
                    his quintessential brother.

Basely decapitated by Arjuna's arrow, Karna
has no need now of the pernicious palimpsest
of his memory which failed him as foretold in
his life's tussle with the Other.
Conclusively, his blood's full fountain reddens
the western sky, spells out his father Surya's
reticence in acknowledging kin when
          it matters most.

3

Peripatetic shadows wend without wincing
now neutrally around us, around the untended
swords, shields, axes,
                    chariot wheels still spinning
                    mad circles in the dust.

After the city falls, in faint starlight
and in the glow of embers, crackling, the wind
pushes through the indelible smoke of old women's
flesh and the flesh of cats trapped in basements;
          it meanders through gutted
corridors and kitchens, flaps the scraps of
bed-sheets on gilded double-beds
                         and flounders.

               In one silent courtyard
                  the moon
                         floats inside the well,
                    a yellow, rusty
                              bucket.

**(Published in *Vyasa's Bheeshma: Creative Insights*,
Ed. P. Lal, Writers Workshop,1992, p.464)**

BAUL, street singer

How could the world's
strange undoing be laid
    at your door?

Old raconteur and guest,
you come but for a day,
    your songs uncurl

through the mist, then
catch like charred
    locusts in your throat.

What summer wind breaks
the night's foreground with
    such a furious lashing?

What crackling distances
grow through your
    monosyllables
        of fire?

ON SEEING TARKOVSKY'S FILM, THE SACRIFICE
"Let us unmask the king as he passes." — Emerson

Prodigious is your fancy, irreducible your fears.
For long muffled hours north windless by the sound,
enraptured in mists that scuttle, you struggle to
rip off a conundrum of masks in epic retrospection,
reshuffle and space the munificent years.

In the choppy metaphysical waters of possibilities
When no dark corner is left to be turned, we having
staked our doomsday turning; when not one promontory
or rock remains to head into, we having done so already
on the black reef of the pride of nations,

your silences in rapt monochrome so suddenly
professed, indented into a newfangled lithograph hoisted
on a tackle and spiked, constitute our day's summons;
come! tell us another one, thoughtful raconteur,
what have you exhumed from your father's porch way ?
What soul's weariness have you so closely pickled
                in this converging season ?

The clouds have an ashen lining, as does the snow,
and the hunched shoulders of congregations, ashen
their sunken faces at land's end or in their propitious
kitchens; their dialogues in the halls and in the adjacent
corridors and beside the broken sinks

are now the stuff of falling waters in the background,
waters dripping with unclaimed words, waters of
the undone world, waters flowing lyrically over
instances of past habitation, abruptly deserted over
gold and silver coins scattered on the floor
and glinting like the bewildered eyes of poisoned fish.

You present silence as bait, Tarkovsky! Green, green
and slaked fortuitous, green, green and coldly blessed,
concealed discreetly in the landscape as your blue boy
                bends to water his tree.

Canary Hill – Rupendra Guha Majumdar

Within this enormous satellite of a room, lost quantum
in space, what infirmity prevails? What blessing
preserves their slow perfidious breathing?
From backstage, driving geese, fair Ophelia enters naked,
nettles in her hair; she crosses the room on her toes,
looks askance, a lost ballerina, still searching
           for a prayer.

Is that not King Lear in the dark blue kimono, dry
tears on his cheeks, running on the grounds, eluding those
who are trying to hold him down on the wet grass
as he sings his newly discovered songs?

You present silence as bait, Tarkovsky, and we,
of course, swallow it, the sea's winter morning whole,
numb and dripping, foisted through the mist, trussed.

Shore and tree, father and son: two pairs
           of ultimate choices.

Must you then, must you, addressing yourself to
The omniscient sender of pink telegrams, sacrifice
         one
              to redeem the voice
               of the other
                      from the oozing, parturient mud,
          so that forgiven,
                 the soul's wind-blown grass
                     may bend
                         curving
                   over the sea ?

LIBRARY WINDOWS
In Arts Faculty, Delhi University

The two squares
of trellised sky
near my right elbow
trace in their pale
countenances the
flight of hawks
a few frizzled tops
of eucalyptus
        spliced
between shredded
cirrus bunched in
arches
    and some
shadows which are
contracted to the
world
       here
            in and
                  out
    of books
measuring promises
       promises

MEMORIES OF A MARCH IN DANDI

Late night thoughts on Gandhi's Salt March at Dandi, Gujarat, 1930.

Serves you right, British Raj
for nixing your table manners!
Did the spanking hurt ?

Could the laundromat reinstate
the white colour of your pants ?
Was your puppy imperial pride
        undone ?
                All your fault!

At Dandi we gave you a taste
        of your
                own salt.

BAISHAKH

The trees and the storm
holding hands, dance in their own
shadows,
        elbowing the noon
out.

Their billowing fabrics
of wind display festooned designs
of falling
        leaves
                curving in a great slant
downwards
          like small birds
                    landing.

And once below
          on the forest floor, form
into receding elf-like footsteps
              of a love
          that was once here
        dancing
      as if
            forever.

ANTONIN ARTAUD: EYELESS IN THEBES

1

Then, consider: only a face so classical or kingly
could be pulverized so soon, in marble of flesh
during a late April warm afternoon of faith, perhaps,
with the butt-end swing of a centurion's spear or
lash of whip by an unseen hand, wielded in ignorance
in the neighbourhood of a Left Bank Calgary.

Only a face like his, flushed countenance of a
soldier-saint, precocious Arthurian Knight, *preus
chevalier du theatre*, with an unwavering blue gaze,
could be so undone and damned, so tried, so twisted into
the grime, into the gaunt truth of the self.

The sun at day's end, steaming like a disengaged
chariot-wheel over rain-wet grass, hurtles down
the valley of Vincent Van Gogh.

Once, the earth burst into fragments, the plague was
here; the earth dissolved in a prescience of cawing.
A mirage persists of the earth's fullness, sand-blown,
keeling with desire, (infirm of purpose and deed),
wafted in the drone of foxes and the frogs' croaking.

Conceived in wombs of volcanoes, the last charred souls
of Van Gogh's crows scuttle low over flushed cypresses
and fields of corn, beaks primed with morsels of
our scavenged horizons.

2

Artaud hunched at his favourite table in the Montparnasse;
or could it be Marseilles? Or, perhaps, Rodez?
Below a domed forehead and warning eyes (as he peers
at you) lips recede into a toothless month, a thin
black wavering line buckling in doubt, pressing another
omnipresent line, a cigarette, and its extension of

smoke which, ascending, sketches his burning portrait
    into the wind-planking of home.

The theater is full. Behind him lunatics rage. Some
crowd the narrow wings: Handyman-barber in the army,
Woyzeck who slits his Marie's fickle throat under
the full red moon; Count Cenci mouths desires which
brook no bounds: Bluebeard *tyrannos*, pilot of death;
and the Marquis de Sade, too reticent at midday,
miraculous midnight usurper of words.

In front, among the silvery breeze of Bali dancers (as
street dogs bark) he discovers his own evanescent
'double' white-haired Theban Oedipus, groping awkwardly
down the aisle; a broken, club-footed king of sorts, self-blinded,
self-banished from his city, cleansed in the blood-stream
of sinning eyes which gravely hollowed may no more witness
or wail or want the texture of hands and faces and thighs,

    but only measure, crossing
                sleep, the deliberate trickle
      of infinite
           darkness.

BHEESHMA'S SACRIFICE

Never understood really why Bheeshma struck
that oath beside the river, pronouncing himself
Maha-bindu-tyagi for good, as the mountain waters

lapped her ankles, sprinkled her thighs she
who on unrecognizable shores had landed
his concupiscent father like a fish.

Never marry? Then
was it wiser to engender the seeds of war-doom
with such passion before the oil in Time's
midnight lamp had ceased to burn?

———————————

**(Published in *Vyasa's Bheeshma: Creative Insights*,
Ed. P. Lal; Writers Workshop, 1992, pp.463)**

ESCAPE FROM STALAG LUFT XVII

A British war movie about escape from a World War 2 / POW camp, that I saw in school days.

───────────────

This night is borrowed from other nights.
the moon has quite left us.
We make good our escape, crawling through
brambles and mud to know the blue unhampered
air; we have in the instance mortgaged our blood,
down payment for the show,
                              and strips of skin
        the barbed-wires tear.

From the tops of their turrets gaunt jaundiced
arms of spotlight grope for our averted faces:
we contend with a blinded Cyclops drunk and heavy,
stumbling across his cave and missing us each
time with a curse, invoking his own malevolent
powers to undo us on our journey homewards.

Yet our souls abide, our die is cast.
We bite the grass, the sand, spit out our prayers
                        into the ears of worms.

The ink-blue woods murmuring engulf us suddenly
In drops of rain, sparks from a million
chastened jackboots now marching into the past.

Are we free ? Is death still lurching loose-limbed?
Is it left lame behind us ?
                       When dogs
       bark abroad,
               does the horned owl
                               sit still?

ARAVALI SUNSET IN HALDIGHATI

The landscape setting in Rajasthan of the crucial battle between Maharana Pratap of Mewar and Emperor Akbar's Mughal forces in 1576

Evening's a wounded warrior
faltering
                down a valley--

blood streaks his forehead
his shoulders too
                are bloody.

By a boulder he pauses his last
pain takes wing ,a lone bird
screaming   truth-spasms of a tale
        over tumbledown hills

NEW TENANT CATCHES UP

1

Having newly rented this house(freshly
painted), I patently await its "messages",
cryptic or sane, in coded hieroglyphics or plain
urban histrionics wafted from the courtyard
through winter mist or shuffling September rain.

It could be a note hidden at an angle
of the banisters or on the wainscot's brow,
neatly folded into fading appeals of syllables
from a past denouement of dread unbidden
              seeking resuscitation now.

Devoid of gaunt furniture, statue or strategic
cacti, these bare floors are shadow-less in narrowing
rectangles, no Ming bowl or stuffed flamingo
            indent the haze.

Yet before my circumspect eyes the air is rife

with fleeting incumbents within this quartet
of white doors — teacher, soldier, doctor or spy,
having forfeited flesh their bodies dispense
no lengthening shadows,

being protracted memories prowling in a cage only
seemingly molecular "but really, many, many light years away,"
as our media's remarkable professor,
                Carl Sagan, would say.

2
Whereupon I see her poised, the woman at the bay
window, pensive, darkly tinted under blue whorls
of muslin and lace looking lovelier than
a moonlit river with sandbanks of pearls and jade
                promontories.

She watches the sunset's smoldering fields,
the sky's flaming forests flicker as bird-wings
ripple over yon valley's deciduous scrub, setting
the day's long boats and rafts adrift[
Her eyes are black swans limpid on the horizon:
her breasts pouting doves so strangely quivering.

I hesitate on the crucial doorstep, my mind's
entity suddenly unlettered of syllables, unschooled
in lessons, a leaf in the loud overriding wind;
I hear my footsteps echo across the flagstones
              of the deserted city.

3
Unrequited love? A last, recalcitrant whim ignored
before a fatal skirmish on a monsoon night? Surely,
a princess of brilliant passions brilliantly neglected!

Am I the only one who has seen her?
Perhaps, the landlord has a bad conscience.

And isn't a conscience too,
                        shadowless?

Canary Hill – Rupendra Guha Majumdar

ODYSSEUS PRESERVED

Not a simple proposition this, surely,
tying up an epic hero, dread sacker
of cities, son of Laertes, to the lone fir-mast
of his ship in the middle of the Aegean
by his own instruction,
                         divine intervention
      notwithstanding.

In the mode of cunning affirmed in the past
in blinding a Cyclops-conscience and escaping
rudely with a new language and name–
                      shall we
then say to such harnessing

that Nobody is lashed discreetly to the mast,
that Nobody yearns to hear what Death can sing
              so purely ?
Shall we then say, Demodocus, that from Troy
        Nobody returned?

TRIBUTE TO HEMANTA KUMAR

His voice, like light-waves from a long
expunged star, took years to reach us,
ascending from corridors of sunken cities
through whorls of weed laced cerulean blue
'til it broke the moonlit surface
in slivers became splayed
     in the slipstream
             of glaciers melting.

No wonder, his songs spoke of new journeys
where the soul, each time it left its
walled courtyard, willfully lost its way;
where the lost soul, wandering, indifferent
to hunger, seized the last premonitions
of passion, answered cities yet standing
above
     the black waves
          of the sea.

YOURS, IRREVERENTLY, THIS SUMMER

God, my heart is a dead brown horse
That you keep flogging down your twisting
Cobbled lanes, dragging it behind your cart !

True, your hard-earned muscles bulge
Rippling under your shirt and you growl
In chaste German in your sleep, always on guard!

But five times already, five times in this month
Of May you have cut me into ribbons! Take care!
Cool your heels! Have a heart! Let me be!
    Like, what's your problem, man!

I too can spout Nietzsche, Spengler, Heraclitus
And Gibbon, and sit with baleful eyes upon
Mount Olympus, devouring grapes and reciting
    "Kubla Khan" in Spanish!

THE HIROSHIMA CLOCK

1

It's now an old clock (if clocks can be
old), past its prime, paint peeling off,
Retarded-green, speckled with grey, octagonal
head on a straight thick neck; no shoulders
or torso—like a bust commissioned by
a puissant connoisseur who knows his art—
a battered face meditating beyond glass.

Perchance, capriciously it was cut out
of a cliff face with rough quick strokes
of a spike gripped with icy knuckles through
one inclement night when all the world waited
        to know
                how abysmal time
                buckles.

Roughhewn, it hung there, ticking loudly,
suspended in the iridescent air for the timely
commerce of meticulous angels who flew
busily by like bees who must, of course, never
        question why.

And suddenly, its thin hands were strangely
twisted and charred and terse like a leper's
who has no fingers to clutch with as he
stumbles down a flaming staircase clutching
        nothing
              with nothing.

2

What is the time, Rock-Face, now, this instance?
Is it eight hundred and fifteen hours? What is the time
        that would be,
unblessed with ashes, unpetrified in the effluence
        of hate-winds?
Is it the time of the morning when deep in

the bracken of a downtown garden a rare Medusa-Pink mushroom
flowers, pushing the good earth apart, wrenching the pubescent air ?

Rock-Face of Hiroshima! Rock Face of Nagasaki!
    One and the same:
Kabuki-mask with singed eye-lashes,
Kabuki-mask grimacing with blood-filled mouth
    above a garland of flushed hibiscus,
Kabuki-mask meditating in the arched silence
    of the praying-mantis;

    one and the same,
             mask and clock, born
    of rock and fire
             a day in August,
a clear morning
        promising journeys
               to blue distances.

3

White, shredded waves bunched against the horizon.
White, shredded clouds bunched against the sky.
Where are the white birds that circled these islands,
    dipping with the wind as they sang
        for their supper?

The sea, like a lone glistening fisherman poised
on a rock, casts its net of ubiquitous mist: it sinks
consummately, low through the ripples and slopes
of waves, the bubbles of tree-tops: bamboo, willow,
rosewood , pomegranate, Queen-of-the-Forest,

settles over earth-bound, sleeping birds carved
    from rock,
        over wide-eyed children carved
    from the rock
        of a cliff-face.

MARRIAGE AND PREHISTORY, ENDNOTES

Nascent anthropologist that she is (primo-
geniture bound), Munia delves into artifacts
of Time, closely wraps in blue cellophane
a femur or ulna or petals of skull-bone
bearing coded sutures that could, Darwin-like,
damn lemur, marmoset or man in seconds.

The 'tools' of her trade are not metal made
with handles of honed antlers of antelope, but are
potsherds and rocks of the intumescent earth,
useful pumice chisels once, rice-bowls, duck-shaped
ladles now freckled with silver lichen in this
brimstone-May when we, novices of excavations, seek

official marriage witnesses who will absolve our
union in retrospect, sign and stamp on court-paper
and form, then assemble our fern-like fossil bones
over millennia and say ,spectacles slipping down
pachyderm noses, ah! This is no Lepidoptera
or Coelacanth pair ,but hominoid, upstanding man

and wife who lived happily ever before, buried
under the sandbanks of yonder Full-Moon River,
exiles surely, wanderers through pine forests
with lapsed passports,
                       lapsed countenances
           glinting
                  with myriad stars
                            of silver-lichen.

III

TRAIN TO MOTHERLAND

To Mother

Mother's awful state
recalls me to her side.
I do the thousand odd
eastbound miles in
a rounded day

riding pell-mell Express
Poorva, wheels clashing
through the May night's
brimming tunnel...

hoping she's still smiling
there above the black
loam of our town's crust,
sitting upright on her
ruffled bed as I enter with
furrowed brow, a beating
heart, some silent
intruder expecting
      the worst...

hoping she's still there to
receive me warmly as I
turn the courtyard corner
by the well, to clasp me
to her chest, her youngest,
dearest son...

to hear the thousand thudding
echoes of those wheels

finally merging
              into One.

Canary Hill – Rupendra Guha Majumdar

DURGA'S BATTLE

Goddess Durga fights a great battle over ten cosmic days with Mahish-Ashura (Bull-Titan) to restore peace in the universe

Far from losing heart in the throes of battle
(sixth day running without a break), he decides
to don the rough autumnal hide, hooves 'n' horns,
tenacious muzzle, accoutrements of the squint eyed
bull, so much larger than life, blazing
recalcitrant fire and with more than one death
to spare by consanguineous, divine sanction.

His carbon-dusk brow is one eddy of frowns, pressed
contours on tide-splayed sands. Being who he is,
demon esquire, he stamps prime forests, caravans,
pilgrim-staked precipices down avalanches,
playing his last, pawn-shop, protean card of grim
disguise to break, then drive the last keen-eyed,
kohl-eyed, definitive goddess into the dust.

Later on, the "bull" epithet would straddle his name:
they would say (in the mythic vein)-Look! There!
He who has demonstrated the bullish role, worn
the bull-attire, demon extraordinaire, *Mahish-Ashura*,
master-bull, bull of many turns, bull-devil of
the Karakorum fen, who cares for none, great gods or men
or women or smart postmodern goddesses too!

But then, a crick in the neck proves fatal.
Pity, he cannot turn his head or shoulders in time
with a flick (as big bulls do if gnats bother)
when her true lance descends with a sharp
rippling twinge of rending deep in-between the collar-
bones into his black surfeited heart
from the most unexpected angle

for which she, in looking larger and high,
standing poised aloft the tawny
feline back, fiery eyed, breathing hard,

                    has surely her charger,
the lion-king to thank, he whose claws
ripped open the end-disguise,
                    held down
          the bull's tumescent breast
                    beneath
                              her foot.

YALE BABY

In 1993 during a relentless snow-storm over the city of New Haven, my wife and I were faced with the worrisome conditions for the birth of our first child at any hour, the need to reach Yale New Haven Hospital two miles away from home.

1

He bypasses his "due date" in March,
forecast by Dr. Reeves. Fourteenth. No
great hurry, still very cold outside,
and snowing. Most blanche New England
winter in a decade, all concurred.

Surely, far better within the cove
of Majoni's womb than riding high,
bronco-buster, all strapped up later in
the car-seat of the Chevy, though that
nice girl from Tennessee may be
at the wheel.

Black sonogram dots of eyes stare
back at me unblinking. Large forehead,
pear-shaped cheeks, hard, midfield soccer
kick: all proof he's more than embryo,
less than precocious puck for all seasons.

Limbs precisely folded like an astral
parachutist's, he procrastinates on
the threshold of lapsed salvations before
plunging head-first into the abyss of
our sleepless nights with a howl.

2

We bide our time, nestle into No.816,
State and Pearl. Large, cubish, red brick
corner house, "oldest on the block", two
miles from the 20, York Street helipad
of his dinner-time landing.
Eighteenth. Above the sea-front the sky
darkens, sways and stumbles, splits down its
sides with a grimace, spine a bow-strung,
wracked vertebrae of lightning. Winds spew

a whipcord of a blizzard down avenues
        of the worn,

ivy-wreathed, Connecticut brow of the Atlantic.
"Storm of the Century!" repeats Channel
Eight with dread as Elm and Maple branches
knocking on our window-panes, freeze. Parked
cars snuggle into the snow like smart huskies
        after a run.

3

Twenty seconds. A blue, unblemished sky. All clear
and sparkling. Sea-gulls saunter like greying
bankers on the Green. Regular checkup for
mom-to-be at eleven. We catch the Q' downtown
bus to the Yale Rep, then walk three blocks. Past
        the swivel doors,

we await our turn. Through the screen darkly
again the stare. Unblinking, Poised within an
umbilical twirl, he reckons it's time. Temporal
sirens unfurl their tongues. We dash home in
Lydia's car to return within the hour
        and clinch

The tidal spasm of pain that birth prescribes.
At quarter past nine, with red lips pouting
through memories of galactic sleep, he meets
us on our grounds without more elaborate stance
        or press comment.

We apologize deeply,
        for the stiff itinerary.
Surgeons gone, left alone, we bow
            to a destiny
                    of loving.

WORLD CUP FOOTBALL 1998: THE GOAL

1

A reigning monarch of
the Ball say, Marcelo Salas,
Baggio or Batistuta pursues it
like one possessed on a stream
of coloured motion of myriad
hues that twists and turns over
the liquid grass and hurtles
                     to the goal.

An acute angle drive —
after superb piloting
through the cutting reefs
of boots and brawn — swings
into the Defender's ken
as he takes the anger
of the Ball upon his chest
in a rainbow of startled sweat.

A virtuoso tackle, a second's
impasse; the tide withdraws
and turns to the other end
with rapid strides ushered by
the sea-gull cries of the referee
(of the nimble toes) who can
afford to take no sides when
either strikes — though only he
can attest the sovereignty
of the blow.

2

In the minutes passing,
muted explosions ruffle
the air as the Ball dances
across wind-blown fountains
from side to side, boot to
boot in great arcs of shots
or straight ground passes

that race the blood's
sedentary trot, the clock's
intransigent shuffle.

Then, well into the second
half, one explosion sounds
louder still marking
the crescendo of a "GOAL!"
The crowd announces it in one
cumulonimbus voice, the referee
too with biting whistle.

The killer Ball is through
and beyond the invisible wall,
on its axis spinning like
a dam-busting bomb 'til ensconced,
          winded in the net.

3

Quite the high-water mark
of a summer song — a Goal!
no author could be prouder
of the outcome of his inward
strife. Whoever's done it, done
the needful — Maldini, Ronaldo,
Suker or Diego, Alessandro
Del Piero or Platini — in
the last breath of the game's
life when all the chips
are down and the time's up.

As sudden and drastic is
Death's own thrust in broad
daylight or midnight squall,
we mortals fear.
Woe to the hapless loser
on land or sea when the Ball
is through between the bars.

The winner takes all for the while —
and there's many a hand
      and tongue to cheer.

SECOND BABY AT ONE AND A HALF

He likes the feel
of fountain-pens
in his new-world
fingers;

his eyes reconnoiter
the horizon of pages
as his bits of doodling
stumble

and slide over
each other like
waves over shiny
boulders

in the foothills
of the Himalayan
mountains.

His monologues are
often inconclusive
in thematic content —
but what of that!

His kind of words
possess the projected
élan of the frontier man

unmindful of the final
call of worlds
    closing in
   on
       themselves.

KARGIL: WAR ON THE MOUNTAINS

The Kargil War of 1999 saw Pakistan and India at loggerheads in the North-Western frontier, it being the fourth incendiary confrontation since Partition in 1947 over the incorrigible Kashmir issue.

1

Still
    spinning anti-clockwise, inclined
twenty-four degrees to the right, our Earth
plays up its given centrifugal role, hurtles
forward on its own axis-heel, day and night
around the sun,
        spitting out
            the indigestible seeds
of bullets
    on either side
        of the cosmic track.

Still shell-shocked the summer air, traduced
the stringent act of breathing in hewed pulses.
Infants, mothers, mothers-to-be, whimper in
the throes of wrested sleep, in makeshift houses
far from their own — scraps of rotten
pinewood, tin-sheets and tarpaulin held upright
and then lashed together with twine, anchored
against the windblown fury of God and Man —
deep in the ransomed valleys of Mashokh
and Poonch, Kargil and Dras.

These hills have borne witnesses to ages
of scavenging: birds, beasts, avalanches of savage
horsemen have spewed from the volcano's mouth
brandishing *Timur-naamas* of death when cities have
laid down to rest, ignorant in sleep, inured to pain,
when the whole world slept soundlessly, when no
time was left for laughter or furious commands
        barked out at dusk with filial voices
and the thud of drums dislodging the dew
on blood-red oleanders and flames-of-the-forest.

2

Are those wolves lurking in the shadows,
eyeing morsels of humanity on a platter of gold?
Now, above the mountain stream's commotion, before
the break of day, shells twist and scream in an extended
diatribe of death. Deserted lie the border villages,
walls and roofs askew; they echo the night-long barking
of dogs that have all perished on a landscape
                      of pained surprise.

Who are you, pale warriors with unkempt beards,
prompted into battle with no cause of your own,
pupils dilated and shifting–like beetles
                            on storm-tossed branches?
What madman has pushed you so mindlessly here —
bulls prodded across ripe fields of corn — to claim
these meadows that many covet
                                though none can fully
or finally possess
                  or ever in this life really shall?

Tololing is back in our hands, Batalik too.
Daily we throw the dice with the cock's crowing
and the bugle's call. We have our briefs committed
to memory in the instance of capture -- our brains
will not bear downloading! Just think. In the chilled,
disjointed trajectory of the wind, the souls of our dead
and tortured pilots have surely undone
                            the Stinger's bite.

Daybreak tomorrow shall measure the last assault
up the hill of the Tiger. The stakes are few
and far between and clear at a cutting price
that we each if summoned shall pay just once.

To recapture what is ours — nothing is lost.
We have some hours left to lay down our cards
as the flame flickers like ravenous birds.

Are you ready to charge in the name of
progeny living and of those in
the womb,
   as yet unborn?

3

The snow, the rolling breath of epic mountains,
descends on every side, impervious benediction
on fallen sons lying in obeisance between
  the boulders
     with arms outstretched above their
  heads, faces down
upon the breast of the Mother —

all listening to the pressing boom of a great heart's beat
across ravine and sky and distant ocean.

Beloved,
   for ever will the flakes of white
   bury the flagrant red
  that blood deploys in spasms
    from the broken sinews
       of the soil?

METRO SUICIDE ON CCTV

     a very thin
line between
body and   soul

take those
furious wheels

on a railway
     track the
woman's head

placed on hold
for just a blinding
second in the

     glint of the
camera eye
        spinning
into oblivion

is enough
   to
      prove it

LANDSCAPE / A SCHOLAR'S TABLE
To the memory of Sisir Kumar Das

We recall at certain moments
of the summer day memories through
a clouded sky:

in the landscape
of your substantial table
viewed from high
stands a clutch of pens
and pencils like icebound, molting
tree trunks biding for spring,

a few terraced mounds
of darkening books harvested
under a rally of storms; and one
peerless, windblown mountain-peak
on the table's horizon — you...

with a balding pate, poised
comfortably in your chair, musing
over a succeeding generation
of peaks along a never ending
range east and west,

womb
of mighty rivers in Almora once
witness of the parturient *bhairavi*
songs of sunrise
a son sang softly
to 'Maharshi' his father.

The inundating brook—your mind—
searching for long-lost dulcet voices in
the woods, still flows
      through our
            bereaved valley.

ELEGY TO A DOVE

I have seen, at break
of dawn, torn feathers on
the floors of houses,
bereft of body or beak
that in the midnight past,
poised on rafters was
a much contented bird.

I did see, at break of
dawn, torn feathers on
the floors of houses, bereft
of body or beak or eye
by mercy of quick
fang and claw of
spotted lynx dispensed
of soul
        and song.

I may see, as yet, waves
before the eventide
rebound against the cliffs'
white brow with the roar
of grace to scatter afar
her ashes now
        on borrowed
                wings.

PAUSING AT TAO HOUSE, DANVILLE, CALIFORNIA
To the Memory of Eugene O'Neill

Long, long after the Gold
Rush he came out West
to California to garner
those nuggets missed by
the mules and the grizzled lot.

The shadows of Mt. Diablo
pressed athwart his rooms in
the house with the red-tiled
roofs called Tao across
the valley and the streams,

paused there amongst the narrow
bookshelves on the walls for seven
years before the mast in Melville's,
Dana's, Conrad's care past faint
cries of continents at war

and much besides to reach
the darkening roots of sycamore
and oak, forged in lightning,
grip the loose black earth
through his crowded dreams.

At the foot of the hill beyond
the barn, the grave-stone of a dog
contains fond memories of a white
firmament of coal-black stars — Blemie,
constellation of the Spotted Hound,

Dalmatian soul poised, unleashed,
to walk the full distance of faith uphill
as it listens to a piano playing on its own accord
the song of the distant moonlit surf
when all is past rebuke and so very still.

Published in the *Eugene O'Neill Review*, Vol.37, No. 2(2016), 271

TRIBUTE TO USTAD BISMILLAH KHAN

**The great *shehnai* maestro, Bismillah Khan of Varanasi,
expressed his deeply eclectic musical lyricism on the banks
of the river Ganges where he lived and died.**

Dawn sees the rose-tinted river
curving gently into the city
of ancient learning, whispering
through his *shehnai* lips a Bhairavi pulse
of pure ecstasy
and pain unfathomable.

He bows to the river, his mother,
his father, his *taalim*;
        childlike he grins
a toothless smile, then mutters in *riaaz*
a *thumri*, a *kheyaal*, a Braja-baashi song,
taps his bony fingers on his knees;

Elsewhere a known Braja-baashi couple
listens intently among the trees,
dances compulsively along!

By sunset he sits on the steps
of Manikarnika Ghat, sips his regular
khullar measure of cardamom tea;
then plays to God and Man alike
his plaintive notes of reed music

that will bear his soul
to the horizon's edge at the bend
    of the river,

like a Bird of Paradise
                breaking
                              free.

IN LIMBO, COETZEE'S MICHAEL K

Remembering J. M. Coetzee's novel,
The Life and Times of Michael K.

stopped
        in the middle of
the tarmac past noon   duty bound
pushing his dying-mother-filled cart
beyond the city walls to the final
resting place she wants
   her valley of flowers
                      he does

not speak out at once his mind
to the cops at the gate; they bark
at him in unison their black pupil-less
eyes of guns turn upon his ribs
stare past each blunted bead
of breath in alveoli ventricle or valve
                      he knows

nothing moves 'til far into
the steaming haze not yet
the cavalcade of tall cacti turned
to the east the field-rat or lizard
in acacia clad
               nor the lone vulture
high up above   in limbo
       nailed to
                the crimson sky

SEARCHING FOR AN E-BOOK IN THE SPRING

1

I open Project Gutenberg dot com place
the name of one Girish Karnad in the precarious
window above left of page and wait for available dope for plays
online, namely *Tughlaq*, for my English class in the spring term
come January *anno domini* twenty and one five,
we are counting the days.

Gireesh? Did you mean 'girl-fish', asks venerable Guten, curious,
bemused; 'garish?' or 'gish' or G(rendel) 'Irish?', he queries,
a Tiresias groping downstairs. How could I reply?
How Girl-fish? Girl one end, fish-tail on the other, as Prufork
surmised to dare about the sweet mermaids singing each
to each while his bald patch shone like the August moon in
the middle of his sand blown hair.

Next — 'karma', 'karna', 'canard'? Perhaps 'konrad' with a 'k'?
like 'kyklops', the apple of Poseidon's eye, praying for recompense?
What would you prefer? His head upon a dish? Is it a heart
of darkness you prefer? Are you now King Minos
musing over a June solstice, with your pet minotaur drooling
for a midday snack in your bone-laced labyrinth?

Take your pick — girl-fish, bull-man, centaur,
golden fleeced goat-boy with flute on Arcadian meadow or even
the Siren girl-birds in our deep blue Aegean who can sing
every homebound ship into black splinters on the rocks
with their lullabies of eternal sleep.

2

"Do you have that in your memory"? I ask Guten the Borg,
all that took place in happenstance
in the not so familiar Deccan turf?
Are you alive to the deed, to the task?
And can I have the substance of my e-book back
and my girl-fish too?
The silence is as loud as the crashing surf.

Birds were dinosaurs once
with footprints on the run, emblazoned
in rock, a stream of printed arrow-heads seeking a heart.

And here's a strange, landlocked bird-form
a bespectacled seer found on Galapagos, named it
Ebok, after its call, as it walked on water, past grimacing eddies,

on the run, point of dim extinction, nay, extinct, a fate
of feathers undone,
mutely calling
unto the last, "Ebok, ebok!"

_____

(Published in *Salamander*/ Boston:No.41, Winter 2015, pp.182-183)

SURREAL SUNSET CARE OF SALVADOR DALI

The tree bows down to the winter
sun descending into the earth.
The cloud bursts into a paroxysm
of birds, Dali's travesty of Mirth.

The river twirls like a bloody
whip upon the flanks of twilight.
The tiger growls from a moonlit cliff,
warning presumptuous *Night*.

RAWALPINDI CRICKET TEST, 2004

India's Cricket Captain Saurav Ganguly won the toss and chose to field, as Captain Inzimam-ul-Haq of Pakistan looked on. India won the Test Series, 2-1.

1

In the third and Final (Rawalpindi) round
of the Indi-Pak bash
we are miffed about the opening pair
in the batting line, the two
                      who are to face
the walloping wind swings
of Shoab Akhtar and Sami without flinching
or detriment to our own vantage
on day One, Wednesday fourteenth.
Phew! Who has the clout?

In Multan *da mitti* and hoary Lahore
the story line was different:
we won the first, lost the second,
both clinched with thumping margins
that raised the blushes on the bristliest
           cheeks,

flummoxed the smartest willow-
scribes writing columns east or west
of the LOC for the extremes
of *Win and Loss*, chastisement
and praise of the two teams in so
          short a breathing time.

2

Consider this! Sourav's unexpected
return following his tumble 'n' toss
and Kolkata restitution, unwittingly
entails the axe for Akash or Yuvi
for the opening slot with —
master craftsman Sehwag.

But out of the blue, surprising all,
the darkest horse turns out to be

our schoolboy keeper, young Patel,
who for the benefit of skeptical eyes
let's loose like Chatrapati Shivaji
Maharaj with his Castilian sword,

slashing the ball disdainfully to every
corner of the alien field in a fitting reply
before he is caught behind for sixty-nine,
his highest score, as Dravid (the Wall)
takes over, with that glint in his eyes,
to make up for past lapses and Waterloos.
His 270 comes pat.

3

For us, the wind-gods have been quite indulgent
on this trip, our sailing's been fine.
Ganguly has expressed no need to bite nail or lip
or to fling off his shirt to make statements
of his inner tension below or above
                        the regular line.

He has been cool, even intently grinning
(when Shoab hit the six). So has Wright.
Not to beat Balaji and Irfan in the display
of gleaming dentition above the angle
of yanked, cart-wheeling wickets. And
      don't forget Tendulkar

who has capsized untimely. Twice!
So what! In the last over he claims
the last word against the Pakistani side
with a googly which Danish Kaneria wants
      to send to the Hoogly*
like an indigenously launched rocket
but which our dear captain catches with
a leap, a bounce, a roar—and the Series
is placed neatly
                in our pocket!

---

* Hoogly: the Ganges River at Kolkata

BOYS WILL BE BOYS

"Militant attack on Pakistani school kills 132 children."
(*Los Angeles Times*, December 18, 2014)

1

As a matter of fact, the last
lesson of the term was
                        very brief
and to the point,
                        peremptory,
pressed by a penal colony afar to
scribble on their skins with
the blunted nibs of hard-nosed
bullets in rapid succession.

They lay down one by one
obeying a curfew of "Sleeping Time!"
on the surface of the earth's
scarred womb, curling to their sides
knees bent, most fitting position
for extended slumber
        through storms forecast.

2

Now you can never say with that
tilt of your pepper and white head
of hair and piquant smile
"Boys will be boys!" for all
        grammar's grounded
into dust, the regular inundating verb
'to be' shunted into the past.

The tenses have turned rogue in
their fragile moorings, the future is
gutted into seedless memory in
the tense called *'future discontinuous'*!
All future that was. Here grammar
        will not work.
    Yet sentences are passed.

3

Boys will no more be
                boys again.
Boys will no longer be. They were
called by the name of *'boys'* once,
gender checked at birth and noted
in the severed umbilical scribble
       of a midwife's diary;

only their names will presume
to be, become, to bind, disclose, break
even in the autumnal shadows of faces
and eyes, ready smiles dissolving
in a monochrome dusk —

Salim, Maqbool, Sayeed Raza, Ali,
Imtiaz, Shah Rukh, Nawaz — names
windblown,
               floating unclaimed
like shredded untethered kites
       from the mind of a clear
             winter sky.

DAY OF JUDGMENT
A debacle in Connaught Circus, New Delhi

Forenoon of September nine —
a capitulation unforeseen; my two boys
touching eight and thirteen witness
a fall, a spouting of occult blood
        they may well remember.

Carried, on a stretcher, I join
the concourse of debility and pain,
my eyes are open wide, I see
the ceilings of meandering corridors
ripple and stretch over my head
towards an estuary of Intensive Care.
Glass panels gleam on every side.

Bottled saline suckles my veins
at needlepoint as they meekly shudder
and smart, turn sore, a bluish green
labyrinth merging into the distant
promontory of my knuckles
        at the outpost of my heart.

Oesophagus confesses erosions,
duodenum too, staring into the tiny
camera eye that delves into the lunar
lesioned landscape of my guts,
searching on and on for a more than
bacterial cause to pronounce
        I ought to live or die

Or briefly in between,
                merely pause.

NOSTOS*

They never thought I was awake
with eyelids half closed
deep within my mossy chamber,
                They never thought.

They thought I was still asleep.
They thought, smirking, I was gone afar
into the forbidden valley from where
few return by dusk up the swelling river;
but that there could be survivors too,
                They never thought.

They believed I was missing. Lost. Dead.
Whatever. And there was no forwarding
address. Nothing in bold Gothic font or italics.
They were sure of my cryptic undoing.

It was the peak of summer. Streets were
deserted. A cat meowed, ears flattened,
hungry as ever. I did not wish to swing
the millennium bell to break the silence
of my passage, my delayed return
that would make up for lost time,
                They never thought.

Maybe, at some point, I overslept.
Which does not mean I must shut eyes forever.
This sleep was in the cards, it could not
be dislodged. It could not... not be.

It spoke to me, in my sleep. It said, do not open
your eyes, do not open the eyes untimely,
do not pry open your inmost eye, pupil dilating 'til
your mouth can speak the 'Word' in full measure.

I hear the wind in the avalanche
recovering its breath in spasms, lungs heaving,
memory-bowed, heart distraught but true.

The 'Word' and the crumpled pages
of sleep go hand in hand,
wait for the final run,
    They never thought.

See! My lips can pronounce the 'Word'.
My mouth slowly turns the 'Word' with the tongue,
like a small, round, rare and bitter fruit.
I could do this. I could speak and bite, pause
and spit, work my sails to the wind
despite every Siren song, and still live to tell my tale,
    They never thought.

---

*Homecoming

CINDERS

Sure, true beauty is there —
Whether it be in First Folio
or flowers or in cascades
of rain-bowed waterfall.

But what will I blindly sing
of the beauty spent, beauty
where it should starkly be
in unanointed king or queen?

On the *Gulmohar* tree
a resplendent bird is flapping
its mortal feathers to be
free while forests burn

to cinders the limping bird of the heart,
the golden cage, my mother's ribs,
which I can count one
by one before I turn the page.

THOREAU'S MAJORITY OF ONE

Monsieur, please
don't deign to laugh
at Thoreau's idea
of the majority of One.

A lone hero
by a forest pond
can often be all
that really matters.

A single fish-bone stuck
In a giant's throat can
fell him to the ground
in a colossal heap

as he chokes
to death and leaves
his army in shock
and completely
          in tatters.

NOCTURNE: THE BUDDHA STEPS OUT

**If a man conquer in battle a thousand times a thousand men,
and if another conquer himself, he is the greater of conquerors.
      — Gautam Buddha, *The Dhammapada***

1

Eyelids in downcast mode,
           decisive as in battle,
the man at the helm of things, warrior still
acutely sure of the way the world's time passes;

unshod you step into the night, in a trice
you give up the seen
      for the unseen,
           the moon-struck future
      for the now.

No one knows of your spring passage,
your breath of fragrant air. Only the dusk crickets
warble staccato tremors deep within your
extended plan, closely parley and pause, knowing
full well a new war is on the cards while the kingdom
sleeps indifferent to the loud chronicles
           of frogs.

Beyond the walls stretch fields of corn.
River Anoma flows into the valley; blue jackals on
their beat nudge the full moon with moist
snouts, howl in unison at myths
         of shadows.

2

Your feet barely touch the marbled
outreach of the courtyard you quickly cross
to gain the final gate of the citadel you
know too well;
         moonlit aglow
the watchtowers, halls, endless corridors,

step-wells echoing footsteps, furtive voices,
the wind-stirred tinkling chandeliers jostle
as you pass recumbent shapes of guards;
you pass grey shut-eye pigeons nodding on
their feet,
        for once untouched, entrenched in sleep
        by the spotted lynx on its late-night prowl.

Ivory white your steed, Kanthaka, caparisoned for
this end, paws the soil by the gate, snorts acquiescence,
bears you quickly to the edge of the forest
from where
        one of your kind, forfeiting
              the claims of birth,
                      never returns.

3

It's late in the gloaming, the moon's quite full;
your dream-eagle soars above the crescendo
of waterfall spray and wind in the gorge as pebbles
fly from under the hooves of your
                galloping war-horse,
        your head
    held high,
crowned only by

        a hovering aureole
           of fireflies.

ODE TO MY FIAT MILLECENTO 1100

1

So difficult it is to pass judgment on an old car's worth —
after many moons of use and misuse on crowded roads
of the capital and on the Grand Trunk Road envisioned by
Mauryans and later, Sher Shah, the *Badshahi-Sarak* many
centuries old I have driven on from Delhi to Kolkata,
and once, pushing the four-wheel barrow a mile past midnight,
     on an empty tank while street-dogs barked.

She came here first from the east, a thousand miles along
the Gangetic Plains, taking a piggy-back ride in a rail wagon,
boarding at steel-town Durgapur, tethered with ropes to the floor
as they do in transport-ships ferrying cars and containers across
oceans, astute vehicle, a gift, shipped across by father with concern.

It's complexion, black, auto pedigree noted in the Bluebook: Fiat
Millecento 1100, 4-cylinder carburetor engine chrome lined
flanks of sedan class with front doors opening outward like wings
of an eagle seizing the air over a fleeting rabbit which dives timely
into its air-raid-shelter burrow under the Tamarind tree.

2

I board a bus for the Old Delhi Rail-Station yard to receive her —
she's laced in silvery cross-country dust, ensconced in the wagon's
darkness among a range of household goods —two teak-wood beds,
Godrej steel tables 'n' chairs, almirahs, ceiling fans, utensils galore —
all appointed to set up a bachelor's Spartan flat and more.

A Murphy radio too with shining knobs; and one green mailbox
for receiving letters that mother wanted to write to me but
could not in the days given to her when the muscles of her deft
fingers stiffened much before the twilight when her time was up;

when her fingers, trembling like her breath, could no longer
grip a pen or spoon or lightly touch the lineaments of her son's
face, its lingering scar on the forehead, a face like mine, truant
                              and slowly fading

like a meteorite drawn into the orbits
of rogue planets of the galaxy.

3

Such an empty and expectant mailbox, transported
from far, resting earnestly in limbo on the back seat
               of the car, complete with latch, lock, and key,
                             painted a light viridian green,
    recumbent (as the train hurtles on);
       the car
                foreknowing her familial shores, familial times,
                as it was, as it should be, a low murmur
                of four invisible cylinders in a protracted breath;

   my black Millecento
      of multiple years, now unfettered and ready to go,
          move on to better climes, no way,
                       no time for tears.

GRAND CANYON, NOTES AND QUERIES

        On the brink of
your primeval canyon
the zany wind-sculptor of
these cliffs twists and
        turns
the lone pine tree
(deeply scratched all over)
into knots of passion.

It pauses,
as you in white cotton
shirt over khaki cargos
and smile,
hair streaming
        walk
into the picture frame.

It holds its breath as you
look into its blood-shot eyes,
sway drunkenly high above
        yon Colorado river

and ask—
        'Hey!
        Besides carving
millennial rocks with teeth
and claw and quaintly
        scaffolding
a buzzard sky — what else
            can you do?

WORDS ARE

Words are
heavy boots on
racks
      chunks of
hide to be dusted
polished laces
hanging on either
side like the thin
moustaches of
Mandarin
      monks.

Words are
launched bucking
broncos in rodeo
rings bent on dis-
lodging cocksure
cowboys off their
backs with a flick
of the spine—
and successful
      too!

Words truly are
flitting fireflies at
dusk replenishing
the slinking luminescence
of the sun
in the unblinking eye
of the Evening Star.

MT. VESUVIUS: A VOLCANO'S LEGACY

These are at left
and right human
shapes skewed
in time bodies
with no trace of
cellular substance
or name to speak of
in league with atoms.

Spouting volcanic ash
reach them halfway
on the slopes to gain
inferno's myriad
blossoms of fire
in a comedy divine

'til acid rain can
curdle their blood
into lime to lay
the spell of seized
motion and sound-
less pain or fear

for this lost
regiment of sculpted
mannequins of
soiled, dispossessed,
bewildered
      yester year

SHELLEY DESCENDING: ELEGY TO A FIRE-BRINGER

Shelley's drowning in 1822 in the Gulf of Spezia by Northern Italy marks the climax of an inclement poetical career.

*

"It is necessary first to consider the nature of belief"
—Shelley, *The Necessity of Atheism*

1

It seems he was (or is, as Ariel) on the point
of denying the Lord God of sermons — not
the Nazarene — calling it "necessity" to state
a certain abstinence of belief, a pressing of
Socratic ways to test and try, garner proof, even
penning a (David) Humean tract about it care of
Slatter and Munday, the bookshop-printers down
the block close to the University College gate.

Displayed in their bay-window where new titles
chide, meet embarrassingly or clash in splinters
of jousting lances on the Green, his few printed
pages see the light of day but briefly, stranded trout
upon the sands all askance and thrashing for them
bubbles of liquid air after the morning tide had
eased its clutch.

His own pronouncements of doubt regarding
the evidence of *primary* sources gear his early
expulsion from Big-League English paradise:
Oxford, Field-Place, Westminster; the inheritance
of a Whig seat, sedentary briefs, a purse of two
hundred (or more) pounds a year. He could
do well if he chose with some of the Autolycan
examples of the elder Bysshe, by casting
a precise anchor on a worthy gendered shore.

Before the summoning of the Man of tousled mien,
caught unawares upon the moon splayed surf, veiled
fictions on the prowl — Alastor, Athanase, Demogorgon,
Mab — withdraw into solitude's dissonance.

In Love's procrastinated cause, more trenchant
sacrifices Venus demands (poised on Botticelli's
fluted shell in the foam of the Aegean), more
thoughts of skylark-sadness in sweetest song.

New subterranean breathings stir and rise from
Sir Timothy's gardens: roots ungrapple in the lower
earth, sift the loam for rough pebbles, shards of glass,
weeds that surely strangle a morning countenance
of light before winter turns on the heels of spring.
At the slow reflex of dawn, blue-black troubadour roses
unpetal with the glint of the kingdom's romance
under the May-storm's late caress, the realm
                       usurped in its manic dance.

From the bronzed hearth a sliver of breeze unfurls
like a tongue, splays dragon-wings, raises its tawny
head to witness the sky cracking over the mountains.
Reborn as the Twister, the Wild West Wind, trumpeting
prophesies (breath of autumn's being), it takes
the new tyrant to task, drags out and down the outraged
ruler, outwitted One — huge, thunder-wielding father,
survivor of purges — down to the Deep.
His shriek sounds like that of an eagle's pierced by
arrows, plunging through the night-swell
       of the last deluge on this earth.

2

Descending to the underworld of Hades, *aashuric* realm
of unwelcome space, is the penultimate necessity
of the Son's sojourn. Very often he goes alone,
wearing no talisman or resplendent mail or precious
garter to see him through. At other times his (deep
browed) mentor walks anxiously by his side, explaining
things, charting the dread expanse, as specters scramble
and cry, clamor for their turn of mutable speech,
                their last rites of burial.

In his own way, cut to the bone, the Hero prevails,
primed for descents through blizzards and glowing embers

to underground caves of subtle discourses. Presently
unbound, free of manacles or of daily intercession
of the condor's beak and claw that had left no sanguine
instance pass, descending still to one quiet shore
in the Mediterranean, the unchained One, pressing
his life-song (a little) further, goes sailing across
the lovely Gulf of Spezia on the Italian coast
                  near Leghorn.

Inviting a brutish fate in the eyes of the storm,
disdaining caution (not caring to pull the sails
down), he drowns without any audible murmur
in the choppy seas.
For ten days and nights as the blue earth whirls,
shoals of fish unmask him gently, peeling
the keen, midsummer tumult of his eyes.

3

He is no prodigal of reverses, no quayside rat
nibbling at the heels of fortune. Consider him as
he is, even in drowning, drowned — a smouldering fire
in the cupped, unsteady hands of waves, carried
down under while the wind rages and the Furies howl
for the blood of sinners in high places —

carried down to the green valley of rippling Sargasso
as had been when Prometheus on his own prompting,
within a fennel stalk had smuggled his first
consignment of fire down to Man's somber valley
                  unseen.
Benumbed,
        desiring no more conquest in the name of place
or passion, the age-old darkness of the nether sea
     waits to die, to cease to be in the flash of lightning
                of his last
                          embrace.

LANDSCAPE PAINTING WITH A PEEPUL TREE BY RAMKINKER

In the scope of the teakwood
picture frame and even beyond, peepul
leaves smudge the sky with them
print-block triangles of lively green each
with two corners
                    rounded off
deftly and one left to narrow down
with a wiggle 'til the tip releases upon
your unwary eye (as you look up with
head thrown back) a drop of darkened
rain.
     Lips open for more respite after

days of thirst; a grim fumbling with
rosaries of Tulsi beads and marathon
prayers to the ultimate Investigator
of Dreams, haloed up high, bearing
myriad names that along with endnotes
for the chosen tale would fill up
an Appendix portion in the concluding
pages of your definitive text.

The leaves are His words of intent
(we are told) inscribed in Nature,
pronounced in whispers and in
the running brooks; and the thin stalk
of each leaf woven into the trajectory of
branches with the wind's full monsoon
concurrence riding by.

As paintbrushes newly awake, feature in
their own ways for once, endorse shades
of death, the branches untether mountains
of clouds, blue clouds of mountains, shrill,
homeward-calling birds, shepherds, flocks,
colours cascading from the shoulders
of the earth-descending sun into the valley
                  of lost flowers;

      --all within the inclement sweep of
a Ramkinkar-landscape in Santhal oils
and local ingredients on a stretched canvas,
six by six, mounted and framed displayed in
a gallery meant
                for passers-by and princes
with no kingdoms or dreams to call
            their own, just the sky
      brimming over with the turbulence
                of Peepul leaves and branches

swaying above
      an almost illegible signature which crouches
      in one corner of the canvas,
                listening
                        to the wind.

EPISTLE CONCERNING A SEMINAL WORKSHOP
For P. Lal

Dear A_____, how are you in these days of reckoning?
And how are the lucent alumni of CU and of St. Xavier's too
In the vicinity or beyond Chowringhee and Park Street?
And how's your dad's old printing-press, Writers Workshop doing?
Just a little curious to know for old time's sake and new
in the pale flicker of fifty years plus!

I have been scribbling some tales and views besides
Lit-crit essays for book-chapters, poems as usual late
into the night; but no book out since *The Hiroshima
Clock* thirty years back; only cryptic lines of verse and worse
in journals like *Salamander, Unicorn, Vagartha, Insight*—

and co-opted anthologies, lean fare I say, not
worth writing home about! Yes, dearly miss our
college guru, your *pater*, Purushottama Lal at such times
when we may have chatted on Sunday mornings over sips
of steaming tea in Lake Gardens about all the poems
                we did not care to write

but let go from our grasp as they tumbled
down the shallow mud banks of the Ganga
        at Hooghly's Outram Ghat, poems to be
or not to be or how to be —
    we would not know; in the sun in the wind
in the memory
           of whirlpools

        tripping like unfettered laughing fauns
                  into the sea!

Canary Hill – Rupendra Guha Majumdar

BLACK DRUMMER BOY AT HARVARD SQUARE

Midday in November: its cold upon the Rialto
of Harvard Square a cowled black drummer boy
is striking out a staccato rhythm of pain using
an assorted, semi-circular repertoire of steel

plates, bowls, inverted buckets on the bare
concrete stage of the pavement he marginally
occupies; he uses his bare hands only for
sculpting tunes of muted footfalls of thunder

into waves of vibrant butterflies seeking nectar.
Nameless multitudes from some Purgatory pass him
by legs pulsating with the beats in choreography,
images of Bernstein's *West Side Story* perhaps

flash through primordial eyes. One young photographer
halts, turns to look, bends down fast on one knee,
left eye shut to aim at her Nikon to shoot the image
of the hooded black figure for all to see, no doubt;

but shucks! He's invisible as all black brothers are
through the wide-angle lens that filters him out!
I stand on one side by the Harvard CO-OP, do
my bit of peering at this scene scribbled between

pavement and thin air, black profile and limb taking
shape as legs in choreography march up and down.
I see the black boy's conical parka hood, an extended
shadow of the Doric triangle above the facsimile pillars of

Harvard Business School high beyond him, peaks
poised over a crackling fault line, a great divide
across land and sky
            beyond a perennial confluence
                of nameless feet.

HIGHER STUDIES

Quite frankly, I'm
        done with
Higher Studies;

but if you insist
    I go even higher,
please instruct me
        how to fly!

BOTTICELLI'S *BIRTH OF VENUS*

**Goddess Aphrodite, progeny of Uranus sans female
womb or care, is born from the foam of the sea.**

All of a sudden the salt waters of the Aegean in a fizz of millennium
blue curdled around his dismembered flesh, potency undone for good, they
thought, to engender more versions of Titans and Furies in needless strife,
sliced asunder with the curving blade of Gaea's scythe
                                    and the son's rude hand.

Yet the memory and will of godly semen persisted askance into the groin,
the cloying womb of the sea — she could not resist the call, the power, the need
no steel could deny the second consummation of earth and sky,
the 'Birth of Venus' in a chanting of windblown rose petals, faint orphic song.

It was the scene that Botticelli saw slowly evolving with his own
dark eyes and traced it in lineaments of sunlight, dew, frankincense
and more — a strange beholding of belated Beauty of no woman born,
created out of the broken flesh of *aashuric* Man
                                      and the wine dark sea.

UPROOTED

Overnight, it's *fait accompli*
before the sun
is up, lightning or no,
any tree can topple —

Sycamore, Neem or
Pine with unclasping roots
dripping beads of black
sod, a devilish sweat

in the wake of bird-cries,
crow-caws muffled in
chthonic echoes from
down-under where

broken arches of memory
foster moonlit voices.

A skull thrown up
from some unmarked
heaving grave on one side
of the tree

      looks at you
unblinking crystalized
black eyes basking
   in your last surprise.

AFTERMATH IN KABUL, 2021

1

Yesterday Kabul did a Troy
without benefit of the sly hollow wooden
horse to assist entry of rogue
Talibans at the end
                  of the night's vigil.

When the time came in the pink
of dawn the gates were opened
from within to welcome them
back after two decades of trigger
happy blasts and bonfire trysts
outside on the wretched plains.

Afghan Prez Ghani flees over the blue
mountains to neighbor Kazakhstan,
giving bloodshed of "beloved Afghan
millions" as reason for his deft exit;
unwelcome there, he runs further west
                  to Saudi shores.

2

Yesterday at crack of dawn
Kabul did a Troy without being
burnt to cinders like King Priam's city;
other bastions have fallen already
to rubble; an unveiled woman, head-bowed,
kneels in the public square, slumps
forward, shot in the back of her skull;
the crack of pistol fire echoes through
                  the valley.

Cities have fallen like ninepins —
Ghazni, Jalalabad, Herat, Masai-i-
Sharif, famed Kandahar; with few
exceptions they allow odd denizens to flee

the whiplash of bullets; others are
executed on the spot or lose their
desperate grip on the fuselage of an
ascending airplane, come hurtling down
to the indifferent breast of mother earth.
.
The sun, a ghostly wraith collapses
in a heap beyond poppy fields as the faujis
closely cradle their guns like wayward
baby sheep who have grown pointed teeth
to devour not grass and mistletoe but
the available food of cornered flesh.

3

Yesterday Kabul did a Troy without
being burnt to cinders like King
Priam's city at the bend
               of the Bosporus;

what was burnt beyond recognition,
encased in smoke and rubble,
was a nameless tall bird in the public square:
all feathers plucked, skinned to the bone,
possessed only of stumps of wings,

               its songs
of freedom stifled in its throat for now
       exiled from the incendiary sky
            and the tall ruined blue citadels
                of mountains.

DOLPHINS IN THE TIME OF CORONA LOCKDOWN

We heard shimmering grey dolphins
                were sighted in the River Ganga
at Hooghly, the water being easier
                to breathe in and out now
during Corona lockdown, they have risen
                from skewed graves to post
unsolicited messages of their own.
                                  Let them be.

Next are these ultramarine mosaic
                dolphins leaping over the wall
in Pompeii which got pressed and veiled in time,
                an unfolding curtain of volcanic ash
descending suddenly upon
                a mob of bewildered faces;

they carry messages too in brick, dust and lime.

                                  Let them be.

GLADIATOR

Tongue-in-cheek
they said   when
in Rome be as
the Romans are.

In the colosseum
the roar of plebeians
rises to a crescendo
as one voice of
unmuted lust.

I live to kill, kill
to live, I have no
desire to serve
the mangy appetites
of lions

while Nero smiles
and strums his last
sequestered syllables
of blood
            and fire.

POMPEII DIARY

Here is the
Corinthian
problem of
both senator
and slave being
in the same

boat same
time in the
shadow of Mount
Vesuvius — Oh!
Nature's unfore--
seen blunder —

is their common
fate of drowning
together at their
prime in a sea
of ashes and

bubbling lava
one midsummer
day in the
ancient sorrow
of an age of
        wonder!

TELEGRAM FROM THE OUTER CIRCLE

Verily, it is a matter of grave concern and dread,
I say, I've not heard from you Ma since you
left suddenly for the outer circle in the month
of May ages back — It's really quite absurd!
And I, this I, was once your favourite son!

There's been no letter or call, no telegram
addressed to me — with thin white strips of paper
bearing typed words of concern in upper case
pasted in parallel lines on a square pink page
stating a message-to-be.

The not so obvious, thus: "I'm farther than
you can think, beyond your clouds, orbiting in space!
My tiny craft has no will-power fuel left to re-enter
the atmosphere on its own, splash into the ocean
of cyclical rebirth, end the *karmic* race!

No fear! When your time comes, you too, my dear
               will leave no trace!"

TO BE A TIGER

Breath on hold, one measured step
at a time the foot-and-a-half alley cat inches
very softly towards what he thinks
       is his rightful prey,
a Neel-Gai deer many times his size
minimized to just a mouthful in his gaze!
          O what a laugh!—

The unsuspecting buck cares not
at all about possible threats to his person,
keeps nibbling his day's portion of sweet moss
growing on the outer walls of my lord's lone
palace, quite indifferent to the day's surprise
        or the question of luck.

Just before lunging at his prey's throat to
tear him apart limb by limb as a full blooded
Royal Bengal tiger would, tomcat decides — and
timely too — on 'Action Plan-B', licking his chops;
and he eyes instead for his purposes of
gourmet élan, straight ahead at twelve o'clock
 the swaggering and haughty
                approaching duck!

ECOLOGY OF SIN

No wonder
     our holiest river
also happens to be
our murkiest!

Cause every hour
       of the day
tons of our darkest sins
without pause
     are rinsed
in its bludgeoned
     turbid waters!

JOAN OF ARC, ENDGAME

1

Just a strapping teenager of thirteen plus
she is, when sleeping in the barn on a bed
of straw — she hears voices from high in her
temple: voices which begin to murmur
fiery truths imbuing war.

Eyes glazed in wonder, she looks inwards into
their pressing summons; she must be up
and about they say, leave cattle and plough on
one side to take up arms and banner of a live
undulating bed of lilies around the name
of 'Jesus Maria,' lead an army onward
                          into the field of battle

Without delay she asks of her king a caparisoned
horse, shield and armour, a gleaming sword from
St. Catherine's altar held high before the cock crows
at break of dawn. She leads from the front,
screaming into the bitter cold, wins many battles,
a strange new force to reckon with.

2

Taken captive in Compiegne, she's bound
to a stake in the epicenter of the marketplace
at Rouen. Tongues of fire crackle around her
like a whirlpool lapping her toes, a garland of
yellow tulips of fire around the neck twisted
in agony, eyes turning to the east, threshold
of a rocky twilight garden in Gethsemane.

Fire crackles from the tip of her sword, threads
the dark clouds together to hold black rain, past
valley and dale, centuries, into another storm—
as she in Orphic guise turns
into jagged splinters of wind and ash and snow
merging with the blood of the native soil

as she, bronzed angel, returns to the plough and soil
       and her warm bed
                     of blessed straw.

IBEX RAM CARES NOT FOR HEIGHTS

He sits back on the mountain's crest
on a less-than-twelve inch ledge
of blue-grey basalt a thousand feet
above the valley, as wild prickly
grass matching the bowed scimitars
of his horns curves against his chest
and tucked quartet
                    of cloven hooves.

The wind faces him straight-on as
his nostrils quiver with the smell
of rain that wafts from clouds below
him; some clouds are above too
like white cosmic buds
                    of chrysanthemums

lingering to blossom before spring;
as he, sitting oblivious
                    on his exclusive ledge
        of twelve or so inches up high,
            chews the cud,

black eyes
           basking in a last surprise.

DODGING

As required —
move briskly
to the left, move
    to the right —

The fast
    approaching
bullet will not
do it
      for you!

LAST SUPPER

If you think you
      can pull
a fast one and disappear —
think again;
      before supper
is through—
    it may be
        your last!

BEAUTY'S BLUFF

Beauty survives mainly
on separatist pain, always
threatening
      to depart
abroad in a mighty huff!

Come storm or rain,
the change in seasons let
it go — don't fall,
      don't fall for
its preposterous bluff!

FINAL HEARING

Don't frown! All
        is not lost!
The court assures
one last
        hearing
before the sun
        goes down.

SKY HIGH FOLIAGE

The seed
        whispered
to its drowsy unborn
        fetus —

Forget me not
When, with green
        leafy fingers,
you caress
        the sky!

ADULTHOOD

But how
        can I, son,
keep saving
        your skin?

When the dark
        tide rises
even the sun
        goes down.

RODIN'S THINKER

Aguste Rodin's monumental bronze sculpture, 'The Gates of Hell' features his famous figure, 'The Thinker', on its top center position.

Perhaps nothing is faster
than the soul's trajectory
from flesh to lucent air when
the time comes to meet
       our goals!

But pray, what use
is this role of mighty speed
when at the end of the day
we flounder in the lower
depths of an Inferno

with nothing palpable to
listen to, ear-buds on, eyes
wide open, unblinking,
precisely nothing at all to will
or to say on the threshold
of the Gates of Hell —

and Rodin's deep-browed
Adamic man of bronze, *Le Penseur*, *
      still unsure,
          still thinking!

***The Thinker**

SOJOURN OF THE MUSE

My ship of ambitious poems sailed
yesterday loaded to the brim
late at night for the distant shores
of New Brunswick in the Northeast
of a rust-red-maple-tree drifting continent
verging on icebergs, seals and high
        spouting whales.

I spoke to many returning swallows
and sea-gulls about the hectic winter
passage as they came skidding by along
the Atlantic breeze, then over Sahara
sands primed with news of worldly woes,
half-baked wanton internecine wars,
        as their wings dipped low,

then up and down to tell me — rest your
mind, your poems are alive and kicking
though exhausted, spent with woe,
battling wave after wave, dark whirl-
pools and gloom laced dens of dragons
        en route —

they had warned: don't be like those fools
venturing into the infernal wild, stay put,
recumbent by the fireside, read to each
other and kin, drinking flagons of ale past
midnight right there 'til dawn re-live
all the Argonautical ballads of golden fleeces
you have sought in vain
        through the berserk cycles
                of your lives.
They had all warned...
        all warned in vain.

CANARY HILL

It was a modest hillock at the edge of the world,
unimpressive as bastions go or towers of silence,
no Kailash Parbat or Mt. Ida** imbued in snow;
or post-deluge Mt. Ararat where Noah parked
his expedient ark with Yahweh's blessings.

Just a small, geological protuberance of a hill,
a mile or two from where our boarding-school stood,
shielded on one side by tall Eucalypti of myrtle species
and orchards of Mulberry, litchi, Guava
and delectable Langra Mango on another.

It would take an hour or so to dare breast the hill-top;
we sat there on warm boulders like quiet, contended goats
with a known penchant for high places; yet took care
to return timely to 'base camp' before the skirmishes of bats
and the weird moonlit litany of jackals began.

No one lived on the hill (in thatched hut or cave) besides
coyotes and rodents of all sorts and lizards that warmed
their bellies on rocks, popping their orange heads up
and down like morning carnations in the breeze;

Or like sentries of a lone fortress, peering into the night for
tremors of alien sounds afar of hostile feet marching in unison
to conquer dusty courtyards and dustier thrones, legacies
of untethered ghosts once rampant in the fields of war.

Bidyut Narain, Bulu, Amitava — all live nearby
in sprawling bungalows beyond lengthening sunset shadows
of the hill; their kith and kin, old denizens of the land;
they know almost all the fables of love and fear the hill

construes for ages folklore of hunting and salvation painted
on mud-wall canvases of Buddhist footfalls here millennia past;
bowls for alms found under rocks filled to the brim with grain,
abundant compassion for those seekers
beyond the pain of separation, disease and death.

Teachers we knew (of one faith) often accompanied us;
they lie close, below the earth's crust, fore-arms crossed on chests,
done with text-book lessons; teachers of another dispensation
at their post, purged in fire ,one with dust and ashes.-
Both kinds held our hands when it mattered most.

The hill evokes their utterances, reprimands and ageless laughter.
The hill lives at ease in a galaxy of its own making,
laced with bamboo, cacti, dhatura, thorn bushes;
lizards poised on boulders still nod their exquisite orange heads
          like carnations
                    in the morning breeze.

PURSUIT

The wind, a sly sudden shark.

The leaves, small scattering fish.

GLOSSARY

Anno domini—in the year of our Lord
Aashuric—Titan-like identity in Indian mythology
Badshahi Sarak-- Royal highway, the historic 1500 miles long Grand Trunk Road from Kabul to Kolkata, in West Bengal
Baishakh--stormy months of April-May in eastern Bengal, India
Bhairavi—a Hindustani classical-music raga evoking the dawn
Bhaang- country liquor
Bhikku-- beggar of alms, like an itinerant Buddhist monk
Braj-bashi--inhabitant of the land of Braj or Mathura, Lord Krishna's mythical domain
Chelas— disciples
Dhatura--conical purple flower (family Solanaceae) associated with worship of Lord Shiva
Elaichi--cardamom spice of the ginger family
Ghat—flight of steps leading down to a river
Gopis--enamored, rustic, female followers of Lord Krishna
Kshatriya-Indian warrior caste
Kheyaal--a vocal form of Hindustani classical music
Khullar--terracotta, dispensable cups for drinking beverages
Maha-bindu-tyagi--great renouncer of semen; one who took the vow of never marrying
Maharshi— the sobriquet attributed to poet Rabindranath Tagore's saintly father, Debendranath
Manu—Archetypal Man in Hindu belief
Multan di mitti--soil of Multan
Nandalala-one of the many names of infant Lord Krishna, here used metaphorically
Nimbu-paani: lemonade
Pince-nez: Eye-glasses without side support by a frame;

Quawwali—a form of Sufi devotional singing in India
Riaaz-- consistent classical musical practice
Taalim—education of certain endemic skills
Thumri—a light form of vocal Hindustani classical music
Timur-Nama: imaginary chronicle of Mongol conqueror Timur
Tyrannos—absolute monarch
Twaiif—high profile, skilled courtesan in the courts of mainly Moghul nobility

BIO DATA

Rupendra Guha Majumdar is an academic, poet and artist, hailing from West Bengal, India. He has taught English and American literature in Delhi University, Delhi and Suffolk University, Boston; he has been a Visiting Fulbright Fellow in the English Department at Yale University in 1981-82 and 1992-93 and Suffolk University, Boston in 2014-15. He has published five books of poetry in English so far: *Blunderbuss* (1971), *Apu's Initiation* (1975), *Tomcat* (1980), *The Hiroshima Clock* (1990) and, *Coda*(2022) His poems have featured in anthologies in India and abroad: *Modern English Poetry in India* ,ed. P. Lal (1971); *Indo-English Poetry in Bengal* (WW,1974); *Vyasa's Bheeshma: Creative Insights* ed. P. Lal, (*1992*); *The Oxford Book of Animal Poems* (1992) ; *The Golden Treasury of Writers Workshop Poetry* (2009).He has translated Rabindranath Tagore's Bengali play, *Roktokorobi* (*Red Oleanders*) into English for the anthology, *The Essential Tagore* (Harvard University Press, 2011); his poem, "Searching for an e-Book in the Spring," was published in *Salamander*, No.41(Boston: Winter 2015), 182; and his poem, "Pausing at Tao House" was published in *The Eugene O'Neill Review,* Vol.37, No.2 (2016),271. *Canary Hill: Selected Poems,1971-2024,* is his sixth collection of poetry in English across half a century.

www.ingramcontent.com/pod-product-compliance
Lightning Source LLC
Chambersburg PA
CBHW052142070526
44585CB00017B/1939